Patrick Lencioni

"Our consistent focus on organizational health continues to provide us with a real competitive advantage. If the world had discovered Patrick Lencioni sooner, there would be fewer complex leadership and management cult theories, and more effective leaders."
—Gordon Samson, managing director, Williams Lea

"We have learned that in order for us to be successful at work, literally saving lives, we need to be healthy. Working through the organizational health material has helped us clarify who we are, what we do, and what kind of behaviors we expect from people. This work has allowed us to minimize organizational politics and has profoundly impacted our ability to carry out our mission."
—Elaine Berg, former president and CEO, New York Organ Donor
  Network

"Our company has grown over 50 percent during the last three years of economic turmoil. It started with the game-changing work of Patrick Lencioni and our focus on organizational health. I spent my academic and professional career focused on 'smart,' with little attention to 'healthy.' We were out of balance; now we are not. The results speak for themselves."
—Richard M. Heard, president, Insight Investments

"We have made Lencioni's methodology core to our long-term strategic roadmap. The results have been nothing short of fantastic. Employee satisfaction, communication, cooperation, and true teamwork have all improved dramatically—ensuring our spot on *Inc.* magazine's list of fastest growing companies for the sixth year in a row."
—Smith Yewell, CEO, Welocalize

"The principles of organizational health have deeply impacted our company and continue to serve as a driving force for us as we grow and

develop. The organizational clarity piece prompted us to become aligned and realize that we needed to make fundamental shifts in many aspects of our business. With determination and consistency, we exceeded all our goals."
—Steven C. Cooper, president and CEO, TrueBlue

"Our work around organizational health is literally giving kids the opportunity to go to college. We finally have the team, the culture, and the systems in place to work through the inevitable challenges we must overcome to achieve our goals."
—Tom Torkelson, founder and CEO, IDEA Public Schools

"By using the organizational health model, we have created an extraordinary and productive work environment. The design and construction industry has taken note, and we have had many outsiders ask what is so special about our approach."
—Jay Leopold, regional manager, DPR Construction

"By applying the tenets of organizational health, we have moved farther forward in the last eighteen months than we had the previous four years. Many of the employees had legacy issues and didn't think we could actually change. We have proved that we can and the group is enjoying the benefits of being part of a high-performing team."
—Lynn Sasser, executive leader, Baptist State Convention of North Carolina

"As a leader in our field, we were suffering from acute growing pains with no end in sight. Since adopting organizational health as the core of everything we do, our business is back on track with renewed energy and momentum. Our staff, our clients, our families, and our bottom line have reaped the benefits of making organizational health a priority."
—Ken Allman, founder and CEO, PracticeLink.com

"Our organization was historically at war. We had a strong business model, but we needed something more foundational. We needed to cut past the history and build a more cohesive leadership team that provided clarity to the entire organization; we needed to build a healthier organization. It has been a journey, but the people in our multifaceted company are now working together instead of against each other."
—Robert R. Auray, vice chairman, Reverse Logistics and Remarketing, GENCO ATC

"By applying Lencioni's principles, our organization's performance has dramatically improved. We are nimbler, more efficient, more cohesive, and able to focus on important challenges rather than the day-to-day minutiae that were dragging us down. This new approach to work is energizing, and more fun to boot."
—Bill Colleran, CEO, Impinj

"The concept of organizational health has enabled our management team to drive healthy behaviors throughout our company, which has supported our growth over the last eighteen months."
—Colin Guppy, managing director, HMD Pumps

"We have always considered ourselves to be a smart company and have never given our health much thought. We recently shifted our approach and have seen a great response from employees and customers alike."
—Tom Sloane, vice president sales, Export Development Canada

"As a group of highly-educated, motivated, and skeptical individuals, it only took about five minutes for Lencioni's principles to capture our attention and subsequently take us on an important journey. We are now a healthier unit, ready to tackle the major issues facing our business. This new approach to work is now a strategic advantage."
—Alfred Foglio, managing director, GI Partners

"Pat's work around organizational health has been truly instrumental for our company's success. It is the foundational underpinning of our new Leadership Institute."
—Greg Serrao, CEO, American Dental Partners

"Our executive team had plateaued and found itself unprepared to meet the fast pace of change ahead. Through the adoption of Lencioni's model for organizational health, the executive team experienced greater cohesion and collaboration which, in turn, flowed down and impacted the entire organization. In fact, an outside rating group declared that our organization had undergone a culture change that would position us for continued success in the future."
—Ricky D. Napper, CEO, Magnolia Regional Health Center

"Lencioni's teamwork and organizational health concepts have focused our entire organization around our mission, allowing us to achieve superior results. All organizations can benefit from these principles."
—David C. Haley, president, HBK Capital Management

"Organizational health is the cornerstone of our culture and provides a blueprint for our company's everyday work environment. We have made critical business decisions—even closed stores—in order to maintain our health. In the last couple of years, we have increased our cash flow, strengthened our team, and set our family of Harley-Davidson stores apart from others."
—Scott Fischer, owner and CEO, Scott Fischer Enterprises

Also by Patrick Lencioni

The Five Temptations of a CEO
The Four Obsessions of an Extraordinary Executive
The Five Dysfunctions of a Team
Death by Meeting
Overcoming the Five Dysfunctions of a Team
Silos, Politics, and Turf Wars
The Truth About Employee Engagement
The Three Big Questions for a Frantic Family
Getting Naked
The Ideal Team Player

THE ADVANTAGE

THE ADVANTAGE

Why Organizational Health
Trumps Everything Else in Business

PATRICK LENCIONI

JB JOSSEY-BASS™

A Wiley Brand

Published by Jossey-Bass
A Wiley Imprint
One Montgomery Street, Suite 1200, San Francisco, CA 94104-4594—www.josseybass.com

Jossey-Bass books and products are available through most bookstores. To contact Jossey-Bass directly call our Customer Care Department within the U.S. at 800-956-7739, outside the U.S. at 317-572-3986, or fax 317-572-4002.

Wiley publishes in a variety of print and electronic formats and by print-on-demand. Some material included with standard print versions of this book may not be included in e-books or in print-on-demand. If this book refers to media such as a CD or DVD that is not included in the version you purchased, you may download this material at http://booksupport.wiley.com. For more information about Wiley products, visit www.wiley.com.

Library of Congress Cataloging-in-Publication Data
Lencioni, Patrick, 1965–
  The advantage : why organizational health trumps everything else in business / Patrick Lencioni.
– 1st ed.
    p. cm.
  Includes index.
  ISBN 978-0-470-94152-2 (cloth), 978-1-118-26603-8 (ebk), 978-1-118-26610-6 (ebk), 978-1-118-26673-1 (ebk)
  1. Organizational effectiveness. 2. Organization. 3. Success in
business. 4. Well-being. I. Title.
  HD58.9.L465 2012
  658.4–dc23
                                                        2011050953

Printed in the United States of America
FIRST EDITION

HB Printing V008502_121718

CONTENTS

For my dad, Richard Lencioni (1936–2008),
who gave me more than I deserved.

INTRODUCTION

This book is the result of an unpredictable journey, one that began when I was just a kid, probably eight or nine years old.

My dad was a salesman who was extremely good at what he did, but I remember that he'd often come home from work frustrated, complaining about how his company was being managed. I didn't know what management was, but I was pretty sure my dad shouldn't feel frustrated after putting in ten hours at work.

A few years later I started working, as a busboy in high school and a bank teller in college, and I had my first real glimpse of management. Although I still didn't understand everything that it entailed, it was clear to me that some of the things that took place in the organization where I worked made sense, that others didn't, and that it all had a very real impact on my colleagues and the customers we served.

After graduating from college, I went to work for a management consulting firm and thought I was finally going to figure out this management thing. Instead, I found myself doing data collection, data entry, data analysis, and a variety of other things that had to do with data.

To be fair, the firm taught me quite a bit about strategy and finance and marketing, but not much about organizations and how they should be run as a whole. But somehow I became convinced that the biggest problem our clients faced, and their biggest opportunity for competitive advantage, was not really about strategy or finance or marketing;

it was something a little less tangible—something that seemed to revolve around the way they managed their organizations.

When I suggested that we look into that, my superiors politely informed me that this was not something our firm did for a living, which was ironic because we were a *management* consulting firm. But I had been hooked and decided I needed to change the focus of my career.

I spent the next few years working in corporate America in the world of organizational behavior or development or psychology—whatever you want to call it. I found it interesting, for sure, but ultimately too soft, fragmented, and academic. This bothered me because I knew that there was something that needed to be more widely appreciated and understood. But something was missing. Context. Integration. Practicality.

And so a group of colleagues and I started our own firm, and I began consulting and speaking about a practical approach to improving organizations. I have to admit that we were a bit surprised by just how quickly and enthusiastically clients responded to our approach. There was definitely a need out there. Over time it became clear that scores of people working in all kinds of organizations, at every level, were experiencing the same pain that my dad had, and they were hungry for a better way.

So I began writing books that took a practical approach to addressing various issues relating to organizational dysfunction—teamwork, meetings, alignment, employee engagement—while my firm's consulting focused on the integration of all those topics.

Demand for those books, and for our integrated approach to implementing the concepts in them, far exceeded our expectations again, and I started to become convinced that we had found that missing something—that advantage—I had been searching for throughout my career. Based on the feedback and encouragement of readers and clients, I finally decided that at some point in the future, I should bring all of the ideas from my books and consulting practice together in one place. That time is now.

Unlike my other books, this one is not a fable but rather a comprehensive, practical guide. I've tried to make it as engaging and fun to read as possible using real-world examples and actual client stories to illustrate my ideas. It's worth mentioning that many of the individual concepts I cover here have been introduced or touched on in one of my eight business fables—most notably, *The Four Obsessions of an Extraordinary Executive; The Five Dysfunctions of a Team; Silos, Politics, and Turf Wars;* and *Death by Meeting*—where I use fictional characters and plot situations to bring my theories to life.[1] For those who would benefit from a narrative approach to a specific topic, I make reference to those books whenever possible.

Because I'm not a quantitative researcher, the conclusions I draw here are not based on reams of statistics or finely crunched data, but rather on my observations as a consultant over the past twenty years. But as Jim Collins, the research giant, once told me, qualitative field research is just as reliable as the quantitative kind, as long as clients and readers attest to its validity. And I'm happy to say that based on my experience with executives and their organizations, the principles in this book have proven to be as reliable as they are simple.

I hope you enjoy reading *The Advantage* and, more important, that it allows you to transform your organization, whether it is a corporation, a department within that corporation, a small entrepreneurial venture, a school, or a church. It's my goal that one day in the future, the simple principles contained here will be common practice, and that salespeople, busboys, bank tellers, CEOs, and everyone else who works in an organization will be more productive, successful, and fulfilled as a result.

The Advantage

The Case for Organizational Health

The single greatest advantage any company can achieve is organizational health. Yet it is ignored by most leaders even though it is simple, free, and available to anyone who wants it.

That is the premise of this book—not to mention my career—and I am utterly convinced that it is true. If it sounds absurd, it should. After all, why in the world would intelligent human beings ignore something that is powerful and readily accessible?

That question was finally answered for me on July 28, 2010.

STOOPING TO GREATNESS

I was attending a client's leadership conference, sitting next to the CEO. This wasn't just any company. It was, and still is, one of the healthiest organizations I have ever known and one of the most successful American enterprises of the past fifty years. In an industry plagued with financial woes, customer fury, and labor strife, this amazing company has a long history of growth and economic success, not to mention fanatical customer loyalty. Moreover, its employees love their jobs, their customers, and their leaders. When compared to others in the same industry, what this company has accomplished seems almost baffling.

As I sat there at the conference listening to one presentation after another highlighting the remarkable and unorthodox activities that have made this organization so healthy, I leaned over and quietly asked the CEO a semirhetorical question: "Why in the world don't your competitors do any of this?"

After a few seconds, he whispered, almost sadly, "You know, I honestly believe they think it's beneath them."

And there it was.

THE THREE BIASES

In spite of its undeniable power, so many leaders struggle to embrace organizational health (which I'll be defining shortly) because they quietly believe they are too sophisticated, too busy, or too analytical to bother with it. In other words, they think it's beneath them.

And in some ways, it's hard to blame them. After years of off-site meetings filled with ropes courses and trust-falling exercises, even the most open-minded executives have come to be suspicious of anything that looks or sounds touchy-feely. Combine that with the notion that corporate culture has been reduced to surface-level artifacts like funky office furniture, employee yoga classes, and bring-your-dog-to-work policies, and it's no wonder that so many leaders have become cynical, even condescending, toward most things related to organizational development.

This is a shame because organizational health is different. It's not at all touchy-feely, and it's far bigger and more important than mere culture. More than a side dish or a flavor enhancer for the real meat and potatoes of business, it is the very plate on which the meat and potatoes sit.

The health of an organization provides the context for strategy, finance, marketing, technology, and everything else that happens within it, which is why it is the single greatest factor determining an organization's success. More than talent. More than knowledge. More than innovation.

But before leaders can tap into the power of organizational health, they must humble themselves enough to overcome the three biases that prevent them from embracing it.

- **The Sophistication Bias:** Organizational health is so simple and accessible that many leaders have a hard time seeing it as a real opportunity for meaningful advantage. After all, it doesn't require great intelligence or sophistication, just uncommon levels of discipline, courage, persistence, and common sense. In an age where we have come to believe that differentiation and dramatic improvement can be found only in complexity, it's hard for well-educated executives to embrace something so simple and straightforward.
- **The Adrenaline Bias:** Becoming a healthy organization takes a little time. Unfortunately, many of the leaders I've worked with suffer from a chronic case of adrenaline addiction, seemingly hooked on the daily rush of activity and firefighting within their organizations. It's as though they're afraid to slow down and deal with issues that are critical but don't seem particularly urgent. As simple as this may seem, it remains a serious obstacle for many dysfunctional organizations led by executives who don't

understand that old race-car drivers' axiom: *you have to slow down in order to go fast.*

- **The Quantification Bias:** The benefits of becoming a healthy organization, as powerful as they are, are difficult to accurately quantify. Organizational health permeates so many aspects of a company that isolating any one variable and measuring its financial impact is almost impossible to do in a precise way. That certainly doesn't mean the impact isn't real, tangible, and massive; it just requires a level of conviction and intuition that many overly analytical leaders have a hard time accepting.

Of course, I suppose that even if leaders were able to humble themselves enough to overcome each of these biases, there is yet another reason that might prevent them from tapping into the power of organizational health, and that is what provoked me to write this book: it has never been presented as a simple, integrated, and practical discipline.

Once organizational health is properly understood and placed into the right context, it will surpass all other disciplines in business as the greatest opportunity for improvement and competitive advantage. Really.

I am convinced that once organizational health is properly understood and placed into the right context, it will surpass all other disciplines in business as the greatest opportunity for improvement and competitive advantage. Really.

So what exactly is organizational health?

I thought you'd never ask.

UNDERSTANDING ORGANIZATIONAL HEALTH

At its core, organizational health is about integrity, but not in the ethical or moral way that integrity is defined so often today. An organization has *integrity*—is healthy—when it is whole, consistent, and complete, that is, when its management, operations, strategy, and culture fit together and make sense.

If that's a little too vague for you (it would be for me), think about it this way. Whenever I present organizational health to a prospective client or a roomful of executives, I start by contrasting it with something more familiar to them. I explain that any organization that really wants to maximize its success must come to embody two basic qualities: it must be smart, and it must be healthy.

Smart Versus Healthy

Smart organizations are good at those classic fundamentals of business—subjects like strategy, marketing, finance, and technology—which I consider to be decision sciences.

When I started my career at the management consulting firm Bain & Company, we did research and analysis to help clients make smarter, better decisions in these areas. No one with any experience in business will tell you that these pursuits are not critical to the success of an organization, nor should they.

But being smart is only half the equation. Yet somehow it occupies almost all the time, energy, and attention of most executives. The other half of the equation, the one that is largely neglected, is about being healthy.

A good way to recognize health is to look for the signs that indicate an organization has it. These include minimal politics and confusion, high degrees of morale and productivity, and very low turnover among good employees.

Two Requirements for Success

Smart	Healthy
• Strategy	• Minimal Politics
• Marketing	• Minimal Confusion
• Finance	• High Morale
• Technology	• High Productivity
	• Low Turnover

Whenever I list these qualities for leaders, I usually get one of the following reactions, and sometimes both. Often they laugh quietly, in a nervous, almost guilty kind of way. Or they barely sigh, like parents do when they hear about a family where the kids do what they're told the first time they're asked. In either case, it's as though they're thinking, "Wouldn't that be nice?" or, "Can you imagine?"

What I find particularly amazing is that none of the leaders I present to, even the most cynical ones, deny that their companies would be transformed if they could achieve the characteristics of a healthy organization. They never dismiss it as being soft or touchy-feely, and they immediately recognize the practical connection between a lack of health and overall performance. So it would be natural to assume that those executives would then march back to their companies and focus a large portion of their time, energy, and attention on making their organizations healthier.

Well, I've come to learn that even well-intentioned leaders usually return to work and gravitate right back to the "smart" side of the equation, spending their time tweaking the dials in marketing, strategy, finance, and so forth. Why would they do something so absurd?

6

Better Light

One of the best explanations for this strange phenomenon comes from a comedy sketch I saw as a child. I remember it being part of an old episode of *I Love Lucy.*

Ricky, Lucy's husband, comes home from work one day to find his wife crawling around the living room on her hands and knees. He asks her what she's doing.

"I'm looking for my earrings," Lucy responds.

Ricky asks her, "You lost your earrings in the living room?"

She shakes her head. "No, I lost them in the bedroom. But the light out here is much better."

And there it is.

Most leaders prefer to look for answers where the light is better, where they are more comfortable. And the light is certainly better in the measurable, objective, and data-driven world of organizational intelligence (the smart side of the equation) than it is in the messier, more unpredictable world of organizational health.

Studying spreadsheets and Gantt charts and financial statements is relatively safe and predictable, which most executives prefer. That's how they've been trained, and that's where they're comfortable. What they usually want to avoid at all costs are subjective conversations that can easily become emotional and awkward. And organizational health is certainly fraught with the potential for subjective and awkward conversations.

That's why so many leaders, even when they acknowledge the pain that politics and confusion are causing their organizations, continue to spend their time tweaking the dials in more traditional disciplines. Unfortunately, the opportunities for improvement and competitive advantage they find in those areas are incremental and fleeting at best.

That's right. The advantages to be found in the classic areas of business—finance, marketing, strategy—in spite of all the attention they receive, are incremental and fleeting. In this world of ubiquitous information and nanosecond technology exchange, it's harder than it has ever been in history to maintain a competitive advantage based on intelligence or knowledge. Information just changes hands too rapidly today. Companies, even entire industries, come and go faster than we could have imagined even a decade ago.

Permission to Play

And so, being smart—as critical as it is—has become something of a commodity. It is simply permission to play, a minimum standard required for having even a possibility of success. It's certainly not enough to achieve a meaningful, sustainable competitive advantage over any length of time.

In fact, I'd have to say that a lack of intelligence, domain expertise, or industry knowledge is almost never the problem I see in organizations. In twenty years of consulting to clients in virtually every industry, I have yet to meet a group of leaders who made me think, *Wow, these people just don't know enough about their business to succeed.* Really. The vast majority of organizations today have more than enough intelligence, expertise, and knowledge to be successful. What they lack is organizational health.

> I've become absolutely convinced that the seminal difference between successful companies and mediocre or unsuccessful ones has little, if anything, to do with what they know or how smart they are; it has everything to do with how healthy they are.

This point is worth restating.

After two decades of working with CEOs and their teams of senior executives, I've become absolutely convinced that the seminal difference between successful companies and mediocre or unsuccessful ones has little, if anything, to do with what they know or how smart they are; it has everything to do with how healthy they are.

If you're tempted to dismiss that idea, consider this. Though I made the statement just a few paragraphs ago that I've not yet met a group of leaders whom I thought lacked the knowledge, expertise, or intelligence to succeed, I've met plenty who made me think, *Uh-oh. The culture within this team and this organization is way too unhealthy to sustain a successful business.* And time after time I've seen smart companies find a way to fail in spite of their sizable intellectual and strategic assets.

Again, that's not to say that being smart isn't important. It is. But if someone were to press me on which of the two characteristics of an organization, intelligence or health, should receive first priority, I would say without hesitation that health comes out a clear number one. Here's why.

Health Begets—and Trumps—Intelligence

An organization that is healthy will inevitably get smarter over time. That's because people in a healthy organization, beginning with the leaders, learn from one another, identify critical issues, and recover quickly from mistakes. Without politics and confusion getting in their way, they cycle through problems and rally around solutions much faster than their dysfunctional and political rivals do. Moreover, they create environments in which employees do the same.

In contrast, smart organizations don't seem to have any greater chance of getting healthier by virtue of their intelligence. In fact, the reverse may actually be true because leaders who pride themselves on expertise and intelligence often struggle to acknowledge their flaws and learn from peers. They aren't as easily open and transparent with one another, which delays recovery from mistakes and exacerbates politics and confusion. That's certainly not to say that being smart isn't desirable, just that it provides no inherent advantages for becoming healthy.

The same phenomenon can be seen in families. Healthy families—the ones where parents give their children discipline, affection, and time—almost always improve over the years, even when they lack many of the advantages and resources that money can buy. Unhealthy families, the ones without discipline and unconditional love, will always struggle, even if they have all the money, tutors, coaches, and technology they could ever want.

The key ingredient for improvement and success is not access to knowledge or resources, as helpful as those things may be. It's really about the health of the environment. And consider this: if you had to bet on the future of one of two kids, one raised by loving parents in a solid home and the other a product of apathy and dysfunction, you'd always take the former regardless of the resources surrounding them. Well, the same is true in organizations.

The Multiplier Effect

Here is another testament to the superiority of organizational health over intelligence. In my career as a consultant, I've worked with a number of great, healthy companies that were led by men and women who attended relatively modest colleges—people who would admit to being just a little above average in intellectual capacity. When those companies made wise decisions that set them apart from their competition, journalists and industry analysts incorrectly attributed their success to their intellectual prowess. The truth of the matter was that those companies weren't smarter than their competitors; they simply tapped into the adequate intelligence they had and didn't allow dysfunction, ego, and politics to get in the way.

On the flip side, I've seen all too many companies whose leaders earned the best grades at the top universities, who possessed tremendous intellectual capacity and had extraordinary experience and industry knowledge, yet still managed to fail because they couldn't tap into much of it. In almost every situation, it was politics, behavioral misalignment, and inconsistency that did them in, leading them to make what seemed in retrospect like obvious tactical and strategic mistakes. Journalists and analysts always seem perplexed by how those executives "could have been so dumb." But again, they miss the point by attributing the bad decisions to intellectual deficiencies. They fail to see that the real deficiency, the one that makes it possible for smart people to make dumb decisions, is a lack of organizational health.

And so a good way to look at organizational health—and one that executives seem to respond to readily—is to see it as the multiplier of intelligence. The healthier an organization is, the more of its intelligence it is able to tap into and use. Most organizations exploit only a fraction of the knowledge, experience, and intellectual capital that is available to them. But the healthy ones tap into almost all of it. That, as much as anything else, is why they have such an advantage over their unhealthy competitors.

> Most organizations exploit only a fraction of the knowledge, experience, and intellectual capital that is available to them. But the healthy ones tap into almost all of it.

Okay, I've already addressed the biases that prevent so many leaders from embracing the power of organizational health. Another worthwhile question that needs to be answered is this: Why haven't more business scholars and journalists embraced it?

Media and Academia

First, organizational health just isn't very sexy, so journalists aren't terribly excited to talk or write about it. No magazine or newspaper wants to run a story about a humble leader who continues to run her

11

medium-sized company with discipline, common sense, and consistency. They would rather tell you about how a brash young entrepreneur is trying to set the world on fire—and maybe himself—with a disruptive new piece of technology or a revolutionary new service. And that makes sense given that they're trying to sell magazines and lure more advertisers. But it certainly doesn't mean their eye-catching stories are more instructive or practical.

Another reason that organizational health has been overlooked by academia and the media has to do with the difficulty of measuring its impact. As I mentioned earlier, trying to identify exactly how much a company's health affects its bottom line is next to impossible; there are just too many variables to isolate it from the myriad of other factors. But again, that doesn't make the impact of organizational health any less real, just harder for journalists and academics to justify in a definitive, quantitative way.

Finally, organizational health gets overlooked because the elements that make it up don't seem to be anything new. And in many ways, they aren't. The basic components—leadership, teamwork, culture, strategy, meetings—have been a subject of discussion within academia for a long time. The problem is that we've been looking at those elements in isolated, discrete, and theoretical ways instead of as an integrated, practical discipline.

It's tempting to downplay this oversight of organizational health by media and academia and, for that matter, leaders, as just another interesting and unfortunate phenomenon of modern business culture. However, the cost of that oversight is extraordinarily high and cannot be overstated.

The Price of Poor Health
Anyone who has ever worked in an unhealthy organization—and almost everyone has—knows the misery of dealing with politics, dysfunction, confusion, and bureaucracy. As much as we enjoy making

jokes about these artifacts of organizational plight, there is no denying that they exact a significant toll.

The financial cost of having an unhealthy organization is undeniable: wasted resources and time, decreased productivity, increased employee turnover, and customer attrition. The money an organization loses as a result of these problems, and the money it has to spend to recover from them, is staggering.

And that's only the beginning of the problem. When leaders of an organization are less than honest with one another, when they put the needs of their departments or their careers ahead of the needs of the greater organization, when they are misaligned, confused, and inconsistent about what is important, they create real anguish for real human beings. And they experience that anguish themselves too.

Aside from the obvious impact this has within the organization, there is a larger social cost. People who work in unhealthy organizations eventually come to see work as drudgery. They view success as being unlikely or, even worse, out of their control. This leads to a diminished sense of hope and lower self-esteem, which leaks beyond the walls of the companies where they work, into their families where it often contributes to deep personal problems, the effects of which may be felt for years. This is nothing short of a tragedy, and a completely avoidable one.

I point all this out only so that we don't underestimate the cost of allowing our organizations to remain unhealthy, and, more important, so that we fully grasp the opportunity that lies before us. Turning an unhealthy company into a healthy one will not only create a massive competitive advantage and improved bottom line, it will also make a real difference in the lives of the people who work there. And for the leaders who spearhead those efforts, it will be one of the most meaningful and rewarding endeavors they will ever pursue.

Okay, here is the next question that has to be answered, the one that will occupy the rest of this book: What does an organization have to do to become healthy? There are four required disciplines.

The Four Disciplines Model

An organization doesn't become healthy in a linear, tidy fashion. Like building a strong marriage or family, it's a messy process that involves doing a few things at once, and it must be maintained on an ongoing basis in order to be preserved. Still, that messy process can be broken down into four simple disciplines.

DISCIPLINE 1: BUILD A COHESIVE LEADERSHIP TEAM

An organization simply cannot be healthy if the people who are chartered with running it are not behaviorally cohesive in five fundamental ways. In any kind of organization, from a corporation to a department within that corporation, from a small, entrepreneurial company to a church or a school, dysfunction and lack of cohesion at the top inevitably lead to a lack of health throughout.

DISCIPLINE 2: CREATE CLARITY

In addition to being behaviorally cohesive, the leadership team of a healthy organization must be intellectually aligned and committed to the same answers to six simple but critical questions. There can be no daylight between leaders around these fundamental issues.

DISCIPLINE 3: OVERCOMMUNICATE CLARITY

Once a leadership team has established behavioral cohesion and created clarity around the answers to those questions, it must then communicate those answers to employees clearly, repeatedly, enthusiastically, and repeatedly (that's not a typo). When it comes to reinforcing clarity, there is no such thing as too much communication.

15

DISCIPLINE 4: REINFORCE CLARITY

Finally, in order for an organization to remain healthy over time, its leaders must establish a few critical, nonbureaucratic systems to reinforce clarity in every process that involves people. Every policy, every program, every activity should be designed to remind employees what is really most important.

Is this model foolproof?

Pretty much. When an organization's leaders are cohesive, when they are unambiguously aligned around a common set of answers to a few critical questions, when they communicate those answers again and again and again, and when they put effective processes in place to reinforce those answers, they create an environment in which success is almost impossible to prevent. Really.

Sure, if those leaders make a catastrophic, completely boneheaded mistake in strategy, finance, or marketing they could sink the organization. But people in healthy organizations rarely make those kinds of mistakes. That's because cohesive leadership teams prevent groupthink, learn from mistakes, and call each other on potential problems before they get out of hand. And so it makes sense that this is the first of the four disciplines that should be taken on: building a cohesive leadership team.

WHAT'S IT WORTH TO YOU?

Imagine two organizations.

The first is led by a leadership team whose members are open with one another, passionately debate important issues, and commit to clear decisions even if they initially disagree. They call each other out when their behaviors or performance needs correction, and they focus their attention on the collective good of the organization.

The second is led by a leadership team whose members are guarded and less than honest with one another. They hold back during difficult conversations, feign commitment, and hesitate to call one another on unproductive behaviors. Often they pursue their own agendas rather than those of the greater organization.

The question: What kind of advantage would the first organization have over the second, and how much time and energy would it be worth investing to make this advantage a reality?

Build a Cohesive Leadership Team

The first step a leadership team has to take if it wants the organization it leads to be healthy—and to achieve the advantages that go with it—is to make itself cohesive. There's just no way around it. If an organization is led by a team that is not behaviorally unified, there is no chance that it will become healthy.

It's kind of like a family. If the parents' relationship is dysfunctional, the family will be too. That's not to say that some good things can't come out of it; it's just that the family/company will not come anywhere close to realizing its full potential.

The importance of leadership team cohesion is almost never overtly disputed, even by the most cynical executives. But somehow, few organizations invest nearly enough time and energy in it, and certainly not with the level of rigor that building a cohesive team requires and deserves. So it's difficult to avoid coming to the conclusion that most organizations either give lip-service to the idea that team-work at the top is critical, or they underestimate what it takes to achieve it. Whatever the case, it's clear that a better approach needs to be taken if they are to eradicate dysfunction from their teams.

> Few organizations invest nearly enough time and energy in making their leadership teams cohesive, and certainly not with the level of rigor that it requires and deserves.

I should mention here that I wrote a book that addresses this topic. It's called *The Five Dysfunctions of a Team*, and it's a fable about a leader who takes over a political, dysfunctional team and works to turn it around. That book provides a fictional but thorough and realistic case study about how a team needs to wrestle with dysfunction in order to improve. I've also written a field guide, *Overcoming the Five Dysfunctions of a Team*, which provides detailed instructions for how to implement many of the exercises and tools we use in our consulting practice.[1]

What I'll do in this section is present a comprehensive overview of the model and provide advice about addressing the five dysfunctions and embracing the positive behaviors that are at the heart of any cohesive leadership team. I'll also use real stories to draw on what I've learned from clients and readers since those books came out ten and seven years before this one, respectively.

But first, we need to get clear on what a leadership team really is.

DEFINING A LEADERSHIP "TEAM"

The word *team* has been so overused and misused in society that it has lost much of its impact. The truth is, few groups of leaders actually work like a team, at least not the kind that is required to lead a healthy organization. Most of them resemble what Jon Katzenbach and Douglas Smith, authors of the book, *The Wisdom of Teams,* call a "working group."[2]

A good way to understand a working group is to think of it like a golf team, where players go off and play on their own and then get together and add up their scores at the end of the day. A real team is more like a basketball team, one that plays together simultaneously, in an interactive, mutually dependent, and often interchangeable way. Most working groups reflexively call themselves teams because that's the word society uses to describe any group of people who are affiliated in their work.

Becoming a real team requires an intentional decision on the part of its members. I like to say that teamwork is not a virtue. It is a choice—and a strategic one. That means leaders who choose to operate as a real team willingly accept the work and the sacrifices that are necessary for any group

> Teamwork is not a virtue. It is a choice—and a strategic one.

that wants to reap the benefits of true teamwork. But before they can do that, they should understand and agree on a common definition of what a leadership team really is.

A leadership team is a small group of people who are collectively responsible for achieving a common objective for their organization.

Any concise definition of such a broadly defined and widely used term is going to need some clarification and further definition of terms. Here goes.

A Small Group of People

So many teams I've encountered struggle simply because they're too large. This is a big problem and a common one. A leadership team should be made up of somewhere between three and twelve people, though anything over eight or nine is usually problematic. There is nothing dogmatic about this size limit. It is just a practical reality.

Having too many people on a team can cause a variety of logistical challenges, but the primary problem has to do with communication. When it comes to discussions and decision making, there are two critical ways that members of effective teams must communicate: advocacy and inquiry. A professor at Harvard, Chris Argyris, introduced this idea.[3]

Advocacy is the kind of communication that most people are accustomed to, and it is all about stating your case or making your point. *I think we should change our advertising approach.* Or, *I recommend that we cut costs.*

Inquiry is rarer and more important than advocacy. It happens when people ask questions to seek clarity about another person's statement of advocacy. *Why do you think the advertising approach is wrong? And which aspects of it are you referring to?* Or, *What evidence do you have that our expenses are too high? And how certain are you of this?*

What does this have to do with the size of a team? Plenty. When more than eight or nine people are on a team, members tend to advocate a heck of a lot more than they inquire. This makes sense because they aren't confident that they're going to get the opportunity to speak again soon, so they use their scarce floor time to announce their position or make a point. When a team is small, members are more likely to use much of their time asking questions and seeking clarity, confident that they'll be able to regain the floor and share their ideas or opinions when necessary.

If this isn't clear, consider an institution like the U.S. Congress or the United Nations, where members use their precious time at the podium making declarations and statements. The same is true in large committees or on task forces within organizations, where people rarely take the opportunity to probe for understanding and clarity, but instead merely pile opinion upon opinion. This inevitably leads to misunderstanding and poor decision making.

If this phenomenon is so compelling—and based on the evidence I've seen over the years in my work with leaders and their teams, I'm convinced it is—then it begs the question, *Why do so many organizations still have too many people on their leadership teams?*

Often it's because they want to be "inclusive," a politically correct way of saying they want to portray themselves as welcoming input from as many people as possible. And as nice as it may sound on a bumper sticker or a flowery poster, it is an ineffective and inefficient way to optimize decision making within an organization. Inclusivity, or the basic idea behind it, should be achieved by ensuring that the members of a leadership team are adequately representing and tapping into the opinions of the people who work for them, not by maximizing the size of the team.

Another reason that leadership teams are often too large is the lack of wisdom and courage on the part of the executives in charge who put people on their teams as a reward or as an enticement to join the company. *I can't give Bill a raise or a promotion, but I think he'll be happy if I make him part of the executive team.* Or maybe, *If you come to work for my company, I'll have you report directly to me.* These are bad reasons to add staff to a leadership team.

The Noah's Ark Management Team

A smallish telecommunications company purchased one of its equal-sized competitors, and in order to placate the executives of the acquired company, the CEO agreed to merge the two groups of leaders into what I call the "Noah's Ark" management team. For every position on the executive team, there were two leaders, each representing one side of the merger. Two heads of marketing, two heads of sales, two heads of . . . you get it. As ridiculous as that sounds, they were convinced it was the best thing to do.

With so many people on the leadership team—I believe it peaked at seventeen—meetings became a mess. The group's ability to be decisive and come to closure around decisions diminished, as you would expect, and executives grew so bored that a few would actually sleep during staff meetings (I kid you not).

Aside from the comedy of it all, what made this situation so fascinating to me was the way in which it was resolved. Executives eventually became so frustrated by the bureaucracy and wasted time that they started asking the CEO to take them off the team! They were willing to sacrifice their coveted place at the table, and report to a peer, just to avoid having to waste their time and energy working on such a large and unruly team.

Ironically, the ultimate impact of the Noah's Ark approach was not an improvement in the morale of the people in the newly acquired company, but rather a prolonged period of transition, denial, and frustration.

When executives put people on their leadership teams for the wrong reasons, they muddy the criteria for why the team exists at all. The only reason that a person should be on a team is that she represents a key part of the organization or brings truly critical talent or insight to the table. If someone is unhappy with his pay or status or wavering about accepting a job offer, the leader should deal with that issue head-on, not compound it by making the executive team larger and less productive.

It amazes me that intelligent people will sacrifice the effectiveness and manageability of their team for a tactical victory. This is undeniable evidence that many executives, in spite of what they might say, don't really understand the importance of leadership team cohesiveness.

Collectively Responsible

This is perhaps the most important distinction between a working group and a real leadership team. Collective responsibility implies, more than anything else, selflessness and shared sacrifices from team members.

What kind of sacrifices am I talking about? Well, first are the tangible, literal sacrifices. These include standard things like budget allocations or head count, resources that need to be shifted from one suborganization or department to another. Making these kinds of sacrifices is much easier to commit to in theory than in practice, because no leader likes to go back to his or her department and announce that bonuses are going to be smaller or head count is going to be reduced in order to help out another department that needs it more. But that's what members of real teams do.

There are other sacrifices that team members have to make beyond these tangible ones, and they come about on a much more regular basis—often daily. Two big ones are time and emotion.

Members of cohesive teams spend many hours working together on issues and topics that often don't fall directly within their formal areas of responsibility. They go to meetings to help their team members solve problems even when those problems have nothing to do with their departments. And perhaps most challenging of all, they enter into difficult, uncomfortable discussions, even bringing up thorny issues with colleagues about their shortcomings, in order to solve problems that might prevent the team from achieving its objectives. They do this even when they're tempted to avoid it all and go back to the relative safety of their offices to do what I refer to as their "day jobs," that is, the work of their department.

Common Objectives

Though this is pretty straightforward, it's worth stating that most of a leadership team's objectives should be collective ones. If the most important goal within the organization is to increase sales, then every member of the team shares that goal. It isn't just the responsibility of the head of sales. No one on a cohesive team can say, *Well, I did my job. Our failure isn't my fault.*

This is another concept that plenty of leadership teams say they believe in but that few really embrace. Most of them rely far too heavily on people working exclusively within their areas of expertise, handing out different objectives to different team members based on their titles and management responsibilities. And while there will always be a need for division of labor and departmental expertise, leadership team members must see their goals as collective and shared when it comes to managing the top priorities of the greater organization.

Finally, if a team shares a common objective, a good portion of their compensation or reward structure, though not necessarily all of it, should be based on the achievement of that common objective. When leaders preach teamwork but exclusively reward individual achievement, they are confusing their people and creating an obstacle to true team behavior.

Okay, now that I've put forward a general definition of what I mean by a leadership team, let's focus on the steps for building a cohesive one. At the heart of the process lie five behavioral principles that every team must embrace:

BEHAVIOR 1: BUILDING TRUST

Members of a truly cohesive team must trust one another. I realize that sounds like the most patently obvious statement ever made, something that every organization understands and values. As a result, you'd think that most leadership teams would be pretty good at building trust. As it turns out, they aren't, and I think a big part of it is that they have the wrong idea about what trust is.

Many people think of trust in a predictive sense; if you can come to know how a person will behave in a given situation, you can trust her. *I've known Sarah for years, and I can trust that when she says she's going to do something, she'll follow through.* As laudable as that might be, it's not the kind of trust that lies at the foundation of building a great team.

The kind of trust that is necessary to build a great team is what I call *vulnerability-based trust.* This is what happens when members get to a point where they are completely comfortable being transparent, honest, and naked with one another, where they say and genuinely mean things like "I screwed up," "I need help," "Your idea is better than mine," "I wish I could learn to do that as well as you do," and even, "I'm sorry."

When everyone on a team knows that everyone else is vulnerable enough to say and mean those things, and that no one is going to hide his or her weaknesses or mistakes, they develop a deep and uncommon sense of trust. They speak more freely and fearlessly with one another and don't waste time and energy putting on airs or pretending to be someone they're not. Over time, this creates a bond that exceeds what many people ever experience in their lives and, sometimes, unfortunately, even in their families.

At the heart of vulnerability lies the willingness of people to abandon their pride and their fear, to sacrifice their egos for the collective good of the team. While this can be a little threatening and uncomfortable at first, ultimately it becomes liberating for people who are

27

tired of spending time and energy overthinking their actions and managing interpersonal politics at work.

If this is starting to sound at all touchy-feely, rest assured that it's nothing of the sort. It's not about holding hands and singing songs and getting in touch with your inner child. It's ultimately about the practical goal of maximizing the performance of a group of people. And it's entirely achievable for both teams that are just coming together for the first time and those that have been working in a less-than-trusting environment for years.

Personal Histories

The first part of learning to build vulnerability-based trust is a small step that is necessary because to ask people to get too vulnerable too quickly is unrealistic and unproductive. While truly vulnerable team members eventually have to get comfortable revealing who they are, they need to start in a nonthreatening way. That's why, during an off-site session, we take teams through a quick exercise where we ask them to tell everyone, briefly, a few things about their lives. In particular, we have them say where they were born, how many siblings they have, where they fall in the order of children, and finally, what the most interesting or difficult challenge was for them as a kid. Again, we're not interested in their inner childhoods, just what was uniquely challenging for them growing up.

> At the heart of vulnerability lies the willingness of people to abandon their pride and their fear, to sacrifice their egos for the collective good of the team.

This discussion takes just fifteen to twenty minutes, and it always works. No matter how many times I've done it with a group of leaders, I expect them to say, "Come on, Pat, we already know all about one another." And yet that has never, ever happened. Some of the people may know one or two people on the team well, but every time I've done this with a leadership team, people sitting around the table are genuinely surprised at what they didn't know about their colleagues' backgrounds.

This inevitably leads to a newly found sense of respect because of the admiration that comes when someone realizes that one of their peers endured and overcame a hardship or accomplished something remarkable. More important, team members begin the process of getting comfortable with vulnerability when they realize that it is okay, even gratifying, to tell their peers something about themselves that they had never mentioned or been asked about before.

In addition to making people feel more comfortable being vulnerable, this discussion serves to level the playing field on the team. There is something powerful and disarming about hearing the CEO of a company talk about being bullied because he was a chubby kid or that his family struggled with grave poverty. As a consultant, I always find it amazing to witness how quickly the dynamic of a team can change after a simple twenty-minute exercise as people who thought they knew one another develop a whole new level of respect, admiration, and understanding, regardless of their job title, age, or experience.

Backstories

Members of an executive team at a large insurance company were struggling with their CFO, a relatively older guy who didn't give his colleagues much freedom when it came to managing their budgets. The consensus was that he didn't trust the people on the team to make decisions, so he felt the need to micromanage them in any situation involving expenditures. The level of frustration among the team, directed at the CFO, had been building for years and didn't seem likely to diminish.

Then the team did the personal histories exercise. When it came time for the CFO to describe his family situation and childhood, he explained that he grew up in Chicago in the 1950s and that his family was really, really poor. He had no indoor plumbing during part of his childhood, and the electrical service in his home was inconsistent at best. You'd have thought the guy grew up during the *1850s*.

After he finished explaining what it was like for him growing up, he did his best to make the following comment in a matter-of-fact way, though his underlying emotion was undeniable: "So that's probably why I'm so tight with the money. I don't ever want to be poor like that again."

The room was silent as everyone digested the subtle magnitude of that statement. It was amazing to watch the executives immediately begin to reassess their attitudes toward the CFO, and a new level of dialogue quickly ensued about the way that they discussed expenses. That would not have happened had they not taken the time to understand one another from a basic human perspective.

Of course, stopping there would only ensure that the trust level of a team would quickly recede to its original level after a few hours or days. The personal histories discussion is merely the first step in helping a team get more vulnerable with one another.

Profiling

The next stage, though deeper than the first one, is still largely non-threatening. It involves using a behavioral profiling tool that can give team members deeper insights into themselves and their peers. We prefer the Myers-Briggs Type Indicator, because it is widely used and understood, and seems remarkably accurate. However, there are other workable tools out there as well.

The key to the usefulness of profiling tools is that the information that is uncovered is neutral; in other words, there are no good or bad types. Everything is valid, and every type of team member is as useful as the next. That may sound like something a kindergarten teacher would tell her students, but it's both true and important. Every person has many natural tendencies that are useful and helpful to a team and a few that are not.

The goal is to get everyone on the team to identify and reveal those tendencies to their peers, both for the practical purpose of having them understand one another and to help them get comfortable being transparent and vulnerable about their shortcomings and limitations. When members of a leadership team willingly acknowledge their weaknesses to one another, they give their peers tacit permission to call them on those weaknesses. Of course, it also serves to validate their strengths.

Sometimes it's during the process of coming clean about weaknesses that the biggest breakthroughs happen among team members.

Myers-Briggs Breakthrough

I was working with the leadership team of a consulting firm. I didn't know it at the time, but two of the executives didn't enjoy working together, and they had a track record of not trusting one another. As we were going through the Myers-Briggs discussion, something amazing happened.

One of the two executives, Barry, read the one-page description of his Myers-Briggs type aloud to the team. Part of that description included the fact that he was a perfectionist, which made him procrastinate whenever he couldn't do something precisely the way he thought was best.

The colleague he didn't get along with, Tom, interrupted. "Go back and read that again."

Barry read the description a second time, and Tom seemed dumbfounded.

Finally, Tom said, "So, that's part of your personality?"

Barry nodded. "Yeah, I'm like that at home too. I don't want to procrastinate; it's just that I struggle when I can't do something perfectly."

"I thought you were just being disrespectful to me when you didn't turn things around until the last minute." Tom was being remarkably honest. "I had no idea . . . " He didn't need to finish the sentence.

The two of them just sat there, digesting the impact of this simple but profound revelation. I could swear that both had the first indication of tears in their eyes.

Finally, Tom said, "You know, I could help you with that if you wanted."

Barry seemed legitimately relieved by both the offer of help and the breakthrough in his relationship with Tom. "That would be great."

And then they stood up, hugged one another, and wept like babies.

No, just kidding. But everything before the hugging part is true.

The Fundamental Attribution Error

This story speaks to a fascinating phenomenon that prevents people who don't know one another well from building trust. It's called the *fundamental attribution error*.[4] As sophisticated and complex as it may sound, it's really quite simple.

At the heart of the fundamental attribution error is the tendency of human beings to attribute the negative or frustrating behaviors of their colleagues to their intentions and personalities, while attributing their own negative or frustrating behaviors to environmental factors. For instance, if I see a dad at the grocery store scowling at his five-year-old daughter and wagging his finger in her face, I'm likely to conclude that the guy has an anger problem and needs some counseling. If I find myself scowling and wagging my finger at my own five-year-old, I'm likely to conclude that my behavior is caused by my unruly child or that I'm just having a tough day.

Of course, this kind of misattribution, where we give ourselves the benefit of the doubt but assume the worst about others, breaks down trust on a team. The best way to combat it is to help team members understand one another on a fundamental level and to give them as much information as possible about who a person is and why this person might act the way he or she does. By doing this, we greatly increase the likelihood that people will replace their unfair judgments with insight and empathy, qualities that allow a team to build trust and goodwill with one another. Or as the prayer of St. Francis goes, we must *seek to understand more than to be understood.* Though that is not always the case, the benefits of greater understanding can sometimes be staggering and immediate.

Avoiding a Costly Misattribution

I was doing a two-day off-site for the executive team at a large and geographically dispersed technology company. Team members had flown in from around the country for the meeting, something they did every few months.

After I finished my opening lecture about organizational health and teamwork, we took a break. The CEO pulled me aside and pointed out his sales vice president, Carl, and said quietly, "I'm probably going to fire him after this off-site is over."

To say the least, I was surprised. The CEO didn't go into much detail, only to tell me he didn't think Carl was a team player and that he was more interested in himself than the rest of the organization.

33

After the break, we did the Myers-Briggs session, and Carl announced to the team that he was an ESTP. Having shared a bedroom with a brother who was an ESTP, I was able to describe his type fairly well: "So, I'm guessing that you don't like protocol, and you tend to blow off meetings and break the rules when you don't think it helps you succeed. You somehow always find a way to make your numbers, but you sometimes piss people off along the way. Your team in the field probably likes you a lot, but the people at corporate think you're kind of a rebel."

People in the room started to laugh nervously at the accuracy of my description. I pushed on.

I looked at the CEO's Myers-Briggs type, ESTJ, and noted that one of the things that bothered his type the most was broken rules and lack of respect for the system. I looked over at Carl and then back at the CEO. "He must really make you mad sometimes."

Carl and the CEO looked at me as if I was a fortune-teller, and now the rest of the room broke out into robust laughter. Based only on my basic understanding of their behavioral preferences, I was able to describe the likely dynamic between these two executives. Carl didn't deny any of what I had said, and the CEO suddenly had a whole new understanding of his relationship with his sales VP. Most important, he could now attribute Carl's behavior to the way he was wired rather than to some attitudinal defect. That didn't give Carl permission to do whatever he wanted, but it certainly allowed the CEO to take a more empathic approach to working with him.

At the end of the meeting, the CEO pulled me aside and said he was not going to fire Carl, a testament to the power of using vulnerability to overcome the fundamental attribution error and build trust.

Too Much Vulnerability?

Some people ask me if it's possible for team members to be too vulnerable with one another, to leave themselves open to being hurt. My answer is no.

To believe that a person on a team can be too vulnerable is really to suggest that she would be wise to withhold information about her weaknesses, mistakes, or need

> The only way for teams to build real trust is for team members to come clean about who they are, warts and all.

for help. This is almost never a good idea. Perhaps during the initial stages of team development, complete vulnerability is not a realistic expectation. But soon after, the only way for teams to build real trust is for team members to come clean about who they are, warts and all.

I suppose that if a team member were to come to every meeting with a laundry list of mistakes and weaknesses, that could certainly be a problem. But the problem, in fact, would be a lack of competence rather than too much vulnerability. Ouch.

Finally, it's worth pointing out that vulnerability is not about a team member using the team as his own private therapy group. There is something uncomfortable and weird about a team member airing all of his dirty laundry in front of the team. A measure of judgment and emotional intelligence is always required, and I've found that the vast majority of leaders understand where to draw the line.

The Leader Goes First

As important as it is for all members of a leadership team to commit to being vulnerable, that is not going to happen if the leader of the team, whether that person is the CEO, department head, pastor, or school principal, does not go first. If the team leader is reluctant to acknowledge his or her mistakes or fails to admit to a weakness that is evident to everyone else, there is little hope that other members of the team are going to take that step themselves. In fact, it probably wouldn't be advisable for them to do so because there is a good chance that their vulnerability would be neither encouraged nor rewarded.

An Invulnerable Leader

I once worked with an intimidating CEO who rarely received unfiltered or honest feedback from the members of his leadership team. At the urging of his head of human resources, he solicited formal feedback from his team in an anonymous survey and then failed to share the results with them for months. Finally, the head of HR convinced him to reveal the findings at his next staff meeting.

At that meeting, he started by reading aloud his greatest weakness according to the survey data. He then paused, with a slightly puzzled look on his face, and said "Hmm. What do you guys think?" Awkwardly, the execs sitting around the table took turns denying that it was a problem, even though the data had been generated by their input alone. Then the CEO read his next weakness and asked the team again what they thought. Once again, the timid leaders, one by one, failed to own up to the data that they had provided. It was astounding!

Finally, one brave member of the team acknowledged that he agreed with one of the weaknesses in the report and that he had responded to the survey in a way that was consistent with the data. After an uncomfortable pause, one of the other members of the team announced that he just didn't see the problem, and he was joined by a chorus of other executives who left their one honest colleague by himself to incur the disapproval of his defensive boss.

Aside from the disappointing spectacle of weakness that took place there, the real impact of that meeting was a clear message from the CEO to his team: *I'm not going to admit my weaknesses, so you probably shouldn't either.* From that moment on, team members avoided admitting their mistakes and asking one another for help. The company eventually spiraled and was sold for a fraction of its previous value. And while journalists and industry analysts attributed its demise to bad decisions around strategy and products, the members of the team knew that those were mere symptoms of the real problem: a lack of trust that began with their CEO.

The only way for the leader of a team to create a safe environment for his team members to be vulnerable is by stepping up and doing something that feels unsafe and uncomfortable first. By getting naked before anyone else, by taking the risk of making himself vulnerable with no guarantee that other members of the team will respond in kind, a leader demonstrates an extraordinary level of selflessness and dedication to the team. And that gives him the right, and the confidence, to ask others to do the same.

Trust is just one of five behaviors that cohesive teams must establish to build a healthy organization. However, it is by far the most important of the five because it is the foundation for the others. Simply stated, it makes teamwork possible. Only when teams build vulnerability-based trust do they put themselves in a position to embrace the other four behaviors, the next of which is the mastery of conflict.

BEHAVIOR 2: MASTERING CONFLICT

Contrary to popular wisdom and behavior, conflict is not a bad thing for a team. In fact, the fear of conflict is almost always a sign of problems.

Of course, the kind of conflict I'm referring to here is not the nasty kind that centers around people or personalities. Rather, it is what I call productive ideological conflict, the willingness to disagree, even passionately when necessary, around important issues and decisions that must be made. But this can only happen when there is trust.

> When there is trust, conflict becomes nothing but the pursuit of truth, an attempt to find the best possible answer.

When team members trust one another, when they know that everyone on the team is capable of admitting when they don't have the right answer, and when they're willing to acknowledge when someone else's idea is better than theirs, the fear of conflict and the discomfort it entails is greatly diminished. When there is trust, conflict becomes nothing but the pursuit of truth, an attempt to find the best possible answer. It is not only okay but desirable. Conflict without trust, however, is politics, an attempt to manipulate others in order to win an argument regardless of the truth.

Discomfort

But that's not to say that even productive conflict isn't a little uncomfortable. Even among the most trusting team members, there will always be a certain level of discomfort associated with disagreement. But it will be a healthy discomfort, a sign that there is productive tension around an issue that warrants discussion and debate.

Overcoming the tendency to run from discomfort is one of the most important requirements for any leadership team—in fact, for any leader. Every endeavor of importance in life, whether it is creative, athletic, interpersonal, or academic, brings with it a measure of discomfort, calling to mind the old saying, "No pain, no gain." And when we avoid necessary pain, we not only fail to experience the gain, we also end up making the pain worse in the long run.

Conflict Intolerance

Early in my career, I worked on a team with a CEO who couldn't tolerate and, in fact, actively discouraged conflict. As a result, his staff meetings were generally boring and not terribly useful.

One day a few of the members of the executive team started to argue. I remember it well because it was the most interesting thing I'd seen happen at a meeting, and because people were finally digging into issues that needed to be discussed. It was uncomfortable, no doubt, as people were finally airing their frustrations with one another about the direction of the organization. But it was real.

Suddenly the CEO pushed back his chair, stood up, and announced, "I don't have time for this." And he walked out of the room.

His message could not have been clearer: *I would rather have boring, ineffective meetings that avoid the real issues than have to endure the discomfort of conflict.* From then on, meetings continued to be a struggle, resulting in poor decisions being made.

One of those decisions, a critical one about product direction, probably didn't get more than a few minutes of discussion at an executive staff meeting. It turned out to be a backbreaker, resulting in hundreds of lost jobs, lost customers, and ultimately a greatly diminished stock price. More than a decade later, industry analysts and former employees shake their heads at the apparent stupidity of the decision. What they don't know is that it wasn't the result of any intellectual deficiency, but rather the unwillingness of the leader to endure the discomfort of healthy conflict and allow his direct reports to get to the heart of critical issues.

Conflict Avoidance

Avoiding conflict creates problems even beyond boring meetings and poorly vetted decisions, as bad as those things are. When leadership team members avoid discomfort among themselves, they only transfer it in far greater quantities to larger groups of people throughout the organization they're supposed to be serving. In essence, they leave it to others below them to try to resolve issues that really must be addressed at the top. This contributes to employee angst and job misery as much as anything else in organizational life.

> When leadership team members avoid discomfort among themselves, they only transfer it in far greater quantities to larger groups of people throughout the organization they're supposed to be serving.

As critical as conflict is, it's important to understand that different people, different families, and different cultures participate in conflict in different ways. All other things being equal (and they almost never are), an organization in Japan will look very different from one in Italy when it comes to how it engages in conflict. And for that matter, a team in New York City may look quite different from one in Los Angeles. And that's okay, because there is more than one way to engage in healthy conflict. What's not okay is for team members to avoid disagreement, hold back their opinions on important matters, and choose their battles carefully based on the likely cost of disagreement. That is a recipe for both bad decision making and interpersonal resentment.

Why would team members who don't engage in conflict start to resent one another? When people fail to be honest with one another about an issue they disagree on, their disagreement around that issue festers and ferments over time until it transforms into frustration around that person.

When someone comes to a meeting and states an opinion or makes a suggestion that his teammates don't agree with, those teammates have a choice: they can explain their disagreement and work through it, or they can withhold their opinion and allow themselves to quietly lose respect for their colleague. When team members get used to choosing the latter option—withholding their opinions—frustration inevitably sets in. Essentially, they're deciding to tolerate their colleague rather than trust him.

As time goes on, they barely conceal their eye-rolling or sighs of exasperation whenever that colleague speaks. For the employee who is being merely tolerated, the treatment starts to feel hurtful and disrespectful, which is hard for that person to understand. It isn't difficult to see how this behavior erodes the cohesiveness of a team.

As an Irish-Italian-American, I seem to have come out of the womb ready for passionate conflict, and I was certainly able to practice it regularly during childhood. However, some of the members of my team at work came from families that rarely shouted or demonstrated outward disapproval with one another. This creates a potential problem. To mitigate it, team members have to be open and vulnerable enough to explain their conflict tendencies to one another and then find common ground. Using a profiling assessment like the Myers-Briggs can be helpful in this process because people's attitudes toward conflict can be shaped by their personalities and behavioral preferences as much as by their families and cultural backgrounds.

Conflict Continuum

When it comes to the range of different conflict dynamics in an organization, I've found there is a continuum of sorts. At one end of that continuum is no conflict at all. I call this artificial harmony, because it is marked by a lot of false smiling and disingenuous agreement around just about everything, at least publicly. At the other end of the continuum is relentless, nasty, and destructive conflict, with people constantly at one another's throats. As you move away from the extreme of artificial harmony, you encounter more and more constructive conflict. Somewhere in the middle of those two extremes is the demarcation line where good, constructive conflict crosses over into the destructive kind.

The Conflict Continuum

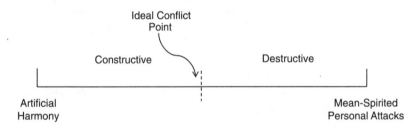

Contrary to what we see in movies and on television, where people go to meetings and argue like battle-tested generals, most organizations live somewhere fairly close to the artificial harmony end of this continuum. They go out of their way to avoid direct, uncomfortable disagreement during meetings or doing anything that would suggest moving away from their comfortable end of the scale. Why? Because whenever they move down the line toward the middle, to that place where they're having more and more constructive conflict, they see themselves one step closer to conflict Armageddon. So they run back to the world of passive, indirect communication and artificial agreement.

The optimal place to be on this continuum is just to the left of the demarcation line (the Ideal Conflict Point). That would be the point where a team is engaged in all the constructive conflict they could possibly have, but never stepping over the line into destructive territory. Of course, this is impossible. In any team, and for that matter, in any family or marriage, someone at some point is going to step over the line and say or do something that isn't constructive. But rather than fearing this, teams need to accept that it will happen and learn to manage it. They must be willing to live through the messiness of recovering from slightly inappropriate conflict, so that they will have the courage to go back to the best place again and again. Eventually they'll develop the confidence that they can survive an occasional step over the line and can even get stronger and build greater trust with one another when they do. But this will never happen if executives are clinging to the side at the shallow end of the pool in the world of artificial harmony.

The Benefits of Surviving Conflict

One of our consultants experienced the benefits of stepping over the line when he was working with a leasing company. He was helping the CEO, president, and other executives deal with some issues relating to compensation and equity. Evidently, changes had recently been made that weren't popular among many members of the team.

At one point during the awkward conversation, one of the top sales execs looked at the president and exploded: "You know, the real reason we're here is that you have simply become greedy and we've become nothing but highly compensated laborers!"

A long, uncomfortable pause followed. The president seemed to be in shock and the other executives were looking at the consultant to see what he would do to salvage the situation. Resisting the temptation to dive in, he let the moment continue so that the team would eventually reengage.

Finally, after a ten- or fifteen-second pause (which felt like two minutes to our consultant), the angry sales exec spoke again: "Wait a minute. That wasn't fair. I can't allow a seven-year relationship to go over the cliff because I lost my cool. So let me apologize and try that again. You guys changed the equity policy without telling us why. It was a change in the rules halfway through the game, and it has led to a lot of hard feelings."

The president accepted the apology, and suddenly the rest of the team started airing some of the concerns that they had been withholding for a long time. At the end of the meeting—and this time I'm not joking—the sales exec went over to the president and gave him a hug. It was a breakthrough for the team, and it would not have happened had someone not stepped over the line—and if the consultant had not allowed them to work through it.

Nowhere does this tendency toward artificial harmony show itself more than in mission-driven nonprofit organizations, most notably churches. People who work in those organizations tend to have a misguided idea that they cannot be frustrated or disagreeable with one another. What they're doing is confusing being nice with being kind.

> Two people who trust and care about one another and are engaged in something important should feel compelled to disagree, and sometimes passionately, when they see things differently.

Two people who trust and care about one another and are engaged in something important (that sure sounds like a mission-driven nonprofit to me) should feel compelled to disagree with one another, sometimes passionately, when they see things differently. After all, the consequences of making bad decisions are great. When leadership team members fail to disagree around issues, not only are they increasing the likelihood of losing respect for one another and encountering destructive conflict later when people start griping in the hallways, they're also making bad decisions and letting down the people they're supposed to be serving. And they do this all in the name of being "nice."

Conflict Tools

Even when teams understand the importance of conflict, it is frequently difficult to get them to engage in it. That's how powerful our cultural aversion is to discomfort. In order to break through that aversion, there are a few things that a team leader can do.

One of the best ways for leaders to raise the level of healthy conflict on a team is by *mining for conflict* during meetings. This happens when they suspect that unearthed disagreement is lurking in the room and gently demand that people come clean. At first, mining for conflict might seem like stirring the pot and looking for trouble. But it is quite the opposite. By looking for and exposing potential and even subtle disagreements that have not come to the surface, team leaders—and, heck, team members can do it too—avoid the destructive hallway conversations that inevitably result when people are reluctant to engage in direct, productive debate.

Another tool for increasing conflict is something I refer to as *real-time permission.* The idea here is that people need to get immediate feedback, the positive kind, when they start to try out this approach to conflict. And no matter how minor the nature of that initial conflict might seem, it is going to be uncomfortable.

So when a leader sees her people engaging in disagreement during a meeting, even over something relatively innocuous, she should do something that may seem counterintuitive but is remarkably helpful: interrupt. That's right. Just as people are beginning to challenge one

45

another, she should stop them for a moment to remind them that what they are doing is good.

That may sound a little patronizing, even childish, but it won't come across that way. What it will do is give people the permission they need to overcome their guilt—and they'll definitely be fighting off feelings of guilt—and continue to engage in healthy but uncomfortable conflict without unnecessary and distracting tension. I've done this with many of the teams I work with, and they are always genuinely relieved to have someone remind them, right in that moment, that they are actually helping the team by disagreeing, not hurting it. Their tension seems to melt away and they're able to focus on resolving the issue at hand.

Another way that leaders can help their teams overcome their aversion to conflict is by creating clear expectations and guidelines around what it should entail.

Rules of Engagement

One of our consultants worked with the leadership team of a division within a large beverage company. He convinced the VP of that division that more conflict was necessary on the team. Unfortunately, they were having a hard time getting people to engage in it. This is typical.

So the VP put in place two formal rules.

First, if people remained silent during discussions, he would interpret that as disagreement. People quickly realized that if they didn't weigh in, a decision could not be made. Second, at the end of every discussion, the VP would go around the room and ask every member of his team for a formal commitment to the decision.

These simple rules changed the nature of their meetings and increased healthy conflict almost immediately. This would not have happened had the VP simply told his team that they should engage in more conflict.

Finally, it's important to remember that the reluctance to engage in conflict is not always a problem of conflict per se. In many cases, and perhaps in most of them, the real problem goes back to a lack of trust. Remember that when team members aren't comfortable being vulnerable, they aren't going to feel comfortable or safe engaging in conflict. If that's the case, then no amount of training or discussion around conflict is going to bring it about. Trust must be established if real conflict is to occur.

In a similar way that trust enables conflict, conflict allows a team to move on to the next critical behavior of a cohesive team: achieving commitment.

BEHAVIOR 3: ACHIEVING COMMITMENT

The reason that conflict is so important is that a team cannot achieve commitment without it. People will not actively commit to a decision if they have not had the opportunity to provide input, ask questions, and understand the rationale behind it. Another way to say this is, "If people don't weigh in, they can't buy in."

This is a critical point and needs to be clarified because it should not be misinterpreted as an argument for consensus. When leadership teams wait for consensus before taking action, they usually end up with decisions that are made too late and are mildly disagreeable to everyone. This is a recipe for mediocrity and frustration.

> When leadership teams wait for consensus before taking action, they usually end up with decisions that are made too late and are mildly disagreeable to everyone. This is a recipe for mediocrity and frustration.

Great teams avoid the consensus trap by embracing a concept that Intel, the legendary microchip manufacturer, calls "disagree and commit." Basically they believe that even when people can't come to an agreement around an issue, they must still leave the room unambiguously committed to a common course of action. Most executives who hear about this disagree-and-commit philosophy are immediately convinced that it is something they want. But they need to remember that it requires a willingness on the part of the leader to invite the discomfort of conflict. After all, the principle of disagree and commit can't happen without the disagree part.

See, it's only when colleagues speak up and put their opinions on the table, without holding back, that the leader can confidently fulfill one of his most important responsibilities: breaking ties. When a leader knows that everyone on the team has weighed in and provided every possible perspective needed for a fully informed decision, he can then bring a discussion to a clear and unambiguous close and expect team members to rally around the final decision even if they initially disagreed with it.

Some leaders have a hard time believing this. They feel that if they entertain disagreement around a contentious topic, they'll make it less likely that they'll be able to gain commitment. But this is selling their employees short. The truth is, very few people in the world are incapable of supporting a decision merely because they had a different idea. Most people are generally reasonable and can rally around an idea that wasn't their own as long as they know they've had a chance to weigh in. But when there has been no conflict, when different opinions have not been aired and debated, it becomes virtually impossible for team members to commit to a decision, at least not actively.

When people leave a meeting without active commitment around a decision, they don't go back to their offices and design a plan to sabotage the idea. That happens only on television and in the movies, and it makes for great theater. In real life, what actually happens is far more boring—and more dangerous.

Most leaders have learned the art of passive agreement: going to a meeting, smiling and nodding their heads when a decision is made that they don't agree with. They then go back to their offices and do as little as possible to support that idea. They don't promote it on their own team, and they certainly aren't willing to run out onto the tracks waving their arms to prevent a train wreck. Instead, they sit back and watch problems develop, quietly looking forward to the day when things go badly and they can say, "Well, I never really liked that idea in the first place." The impact of this is often embarrassing and costly for the organization.

The Price of Passivity

The leadership team at an international pharmaceutical company realized that its sales were beginning to decline and that its expenses were heading in the opposite direction. During a staff meeting, the CEO decided that in an effort to curb costs, a moratorium would be placed on all first-class and business-class air travel. This would not be easy for people who traveled frequently and far.

As usual, no debate was encouraged among the team. Executives simply nodded their heads in agreement, something the CEO was all too happy to accept as commitment.

Well, half of the executives at the meeting went to their teams and gave them the unpopular order to change the way they traveled. The other half told their staff members to ignore the decree. When people in the organization started to notice the discrepancy in behavior among departments, anger and frustration broke out.

Employees in the obedient departments were upset at their respective leaders for holding them to a higher and more difficult standard than their peers in other parts of the organization. Those leaders were mad at their colleagues on the executive team who had ignored the supposed agreement.

The cost of not achieving real commitment—a result of not engaging in healthy conflict—was undeniable. Forget about the financial cost of people continuing to fly business class. It pales in comparison to the loss in credibility that executives encountered and the internal politics that they created because they failed to achieve real, active commitment around a decision.

The only way to prevent passive sabotage is for leaders to demand conflict from their team members and to let them know that they are going to be held accountable for doing whatever the team ultimately decides.

Specific Agreements

I've always been amazed that even teams that embrace conflict and honest debate can still struggle with commitment. That's because they fall short of arriving at specific agreements at the end of their discussions. Although they are sitting in the same room and speaking the same language, they often leave with different ideas about what was just decided. There is only one way I know to prevent this.

At the end of every meeting, cohesive teams must take a few minutes to ensure that everyone sitting at the table is walking away with the same understanding about what has been agreed to and what they are committed to do. Unfortunately, people are usually eager to leave the room when a meeting is coming to a close, and so they are more than susceptible to tolerating a little ambiguity. That's why functional teams maintain the discipline to review their commitments and stick around long enough to clarify anything that isn't crystal clear.

A good way to ensure that people take this process seriously is to demand that they go back to their teams after the meeting and communicate exactly what was agreed on. When team members know that they are going to have to stand in front of the people they lead and vouch for a decision, they are much more likely to push back on that decision if they don't understand it or don't agree with it. As painful as this may be to a group of executives who are more than ready to get out of a meeting, the only thing more painful than taking additional time to get clarity and commitment is going out into the organization with a confusing and misaligned message.

Misalignment Nightmare

One of our consultants worked with the leadership team of an information technology organization to clarify the department's core purpose and values. After the meeting, the consultant encouraged the team to keep working until they were crystal clear with one another about the purpose and values before doing any communication to the rest of the organization.

The team promised to meet again later to iron out any possible inconsistencies. Unfortunately, they never got around to doing that and decided to go ahead and have a big rollout meeting to unveil the new purpose and values to the more than fifty managers who worked for them.

At that meeting, a handful of leaders from the executive team began the presentation and were quickly met with push-back around their ideas. Unfortunately, that push-back came not from one of the fifty managers but from a member of the executive team who decided to announce that he never really liked or bought into what was being presented.

The people in the room were dumbfounded. Not only did the executive team's failure to get commitment negate the impact of the work they had done, it also caused them to lose credibility among the people they were trying to lead. "We looked foolish, and rightly so," admitted the leader of the executive team. "We couldn't even agree among ourselves, and we were out there asking the rest of the organization to get on board. I vowed that it would never happen again."

After the next executive off-site meeting, the team insisted on getting completely clear about the commitments they were making. And when they communicated to the larger group, not only did they demonstrate alignment, but they modeled vulnerability by acknowledging the dysfunction of what had happened before and the steps they would take to prevent it in the future.

Although few would doubt the importance of achieving active and clear commitment at the end of a discussion, many don't really think about the practical reason that that is so critical. It's only when people know that their peers have completely bought in to a decision that they will have the courage to embrace the fourth and most difficult behavior of a cohesive team: accountability.

BEHAVIOR 4: EMBRACING ACCOUNTABILITY

Even well-intentioned members of a team need to be held accountable if a team is going to stick to its decisions and accomplish its goals. In some cases, people will deviate from a plan or a decision knowingly, tempted to do something that is in their individual best interest but not that of the team. In other cases, people will stray without realizing it, getting distracted or caught up in the pushes and pulls of daily work. In either case, it's the job of the team to call those people out and keep them in line.

Of course, people aren't going to be willing to do this if they have doubts about whether their peers bought into—really bought into—the decisions that were made. That's why commitment is so important. When colleagues know that there has been only passive commitment around a decision, they aren't going to feel good about confronting a peer about their behavior. Nor should they. After all, if a person never really bought into something, why would she heed a reminder from a peer who points out her deviation?

Peer Pressure

Notice that I'm focused here on peers. That's because peer-to-peer accountability is the primary and most effective source of accountability on the leadership team of a healthy organization. Most people assume that the leader of an executive team should be the primary source of accountability—and that's the norm in most unhealthy organizations—but it isn't efficient or practical, and it makes little sense.

> Peer-to-peer accountability is the primary and most effective source of accountability on a leadership team.

When members of a team go to their leader whenever they see a peer deviate from a commitment that was made, they create a perfect environment for distraction and politics. Colleagues start to wonder who ratted them out, they get resentful of one another, and the team leader finds herself being constantly pulled into situations that could be more quickly and productively solved without her.

When team members know that their colleagues are truly committed to something, they can confront one another about issues without fearing defensiveness or backlash. After all, they're merely helping someone get back on track or seeking clarity about something that doesn't seem right. And the person being questioned about her behavior or performance will be willing to admit that she has inadvertently lost her way—after all, she's vulnerable—and adjust her behavior accordingly.

I realize that people who are used to working on noncohesive teams will think all of this sounds like a fairy tale. To those who have experienced the reality of cohesive teams, it is simply the most effective way to keep one another focused on what matters most.

Accountability in Action

One of our consultants was working with a leadership team that had been together for less than a year and had not met in person with one another for a number of months. Inevitably, things were a little rocky.

During an off-site meeting, our consultant led them through an accountability exercise that calls for team members to confront one another about each other's behaviors. The exercise, which isn't as scary as it sounds, usually takes about an hour. But in this case, because the team had not been together for so long and because they had made a major commitment to holding one another accountable, the session lasted three hours.

Among the comments made during the exercise were these: "You need to keep standing up to the CEO and not letting him off the hook when he resorts to unilateral decision making." "You're involving me in conversations that I don't need to be involved in. Just go directly to my reports and get what you need." "Your reports are not telling you this, but your sarcastic humor is offensive to them and it's hurting your team." "You're complaining about me to your peers, but you're not coming to me directly. That's hurting all of us." "Watch out for your self-righteous attitude. It shuts down our brainstorming."

During those three hours, there was some tension, no doubt. But there was also a lot of listening, and even laughter. Most important, there was no hesitation in speaking up. And though the session took a long time, the team was able to repair much of the trust that they had lost over the months that they hadn't been together, and they proved to themselves that they were committed to working together as a functional team going forward.

Overcoming the "Wuss" Factor

The irony of all this is that the only way for a team to develop a true culture of peer-to-peer accountability is for the leader to demonstrate that she is willing to confront difficult situations and hold people accountable herself. That's right. The leader of the team, though not the primary source of accountability, will always be the ultimate arbiter of it. If she is reluctant to play that role—if she is a wuss who constantly balks when it's time to call someone on their behavior or performance—then the rest of the team is not going to do their part. This makes sense. Why would a team member want to confront a colleague about an issue when the team leader isn't willing to and is probably going to let them off the hook anyway?

So—and here is the irony—the more comfortable a leader is holding people on a team accountable, the less likely she is to be asked to do so. The less likely she is to confront people, the more she'll be called on to do it by subordinates who aren't willing to do her dirty work for her. I know this because I struggle with holding people accountable, and I am fully aware that the reluctance of my staff members to do so with one another is a simple function of my behavior. (I'm working on it.)

Many leaders struggle with accountability but don't know it. Some will tell me that since they aren't afraid to fire people, they must not have an accountability problem. Of course, this is misguided. Firing someone is not necessarily a sign of accountability, but is often the last act of cowardice for a leader who doesn't know how or isn't willing to hold people accountable.

At its core, accountability is about having the courage to confront someone about their deficiencies and then to stand in the moment and deal with their reaction, which may not be pleasant. It is a selfless act, one rooted in a word that I don't use lightly in a business book: *love*. To hold someone accountable is to care about them enough to risk having them blame you for pointing out their deficiencies.

> To hold someone accountable is to care about them enough to risk having them blame you for pointing out their deficiencies.

Unfortunately, it is far more natural, and common, for leaders to avoid holding people accountable. It is one of the biggest obstacles I find preventing teams, and the companies they lead, from reaching their full potential. It's no surprise that among the teams that complete our Five Dysfunctions of a Team Assessment (see "The Universal Challenge of Peer Accountability" sidebar), the lowest scores are usually found in the area of accountability.

THE UNIVERSAL CHALLENGE OF
PEER ACCOUNTABILITY

The Table Group has identified a major trend plaguing teams today: team members readily avoid holding their peers accountable for both their performance and behaviors that might hurt the team. The trend is a conclusion based on data collected from The Table Group's Online Team Assessment, a thirty-eight-question online tool that measures a team's likely susceptibility to the five dysfunctions. In reviewing the 12,000 teams who have taken the online assessment, data shows a full 65% of teams scored "red" on accountability—or lowest on The Table Group's three-tiered rating scale of green-yellow-red. Other red scores for the remaining four behaviors include trust (40%), conflict (36%), commitment (22%), and results (27%).

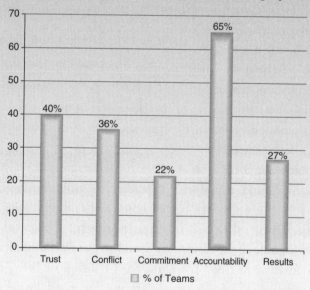

Percentage of Teams Scoring in Lowest Category

Many leaders who struggle with this (again, I'm one of them) will try to convince themselves that their reluctance is a product of their kindness; they just don't want to make their employees feel bad. But an honest reassessment of their motivation will allow them to admit that they are the ones who don't want to feel bad and that failing to hold someone accountable is ultimately an act of selfishness.

After all, there is nothing noble about withholding information that can help an employee improve. Eventually that employee's lack of improvement is going to come back to haunt him in a performance review or when he is let go. And I'm pretty sure there is nothing kind about firing someone who has not been confronted about his performance.

Behaviors Versus Measurables

Some leaders don't realize they have an accountability problem because they are more than comfortable confronting people about issues regarding measurable performance. For instance, when a direct report misses his sales target four quarters in a row or doesn't deliver a product on time and according to specifications, leaders have no problem telling him and taking action. That is indeed one form of accountability, but it's not the most important kind. The kind that is more fundamental, important, and difficult is about behavior.

After all, even the most reluctant, fearful leaders can usually summon the courage to tell someone that he missed his number. That is a relatively objective, nonjudgmental act, which makes it safe and free from emotion. Confronting someone about their behavior is a different matter. It involves a judgment call that is more likely to provoke a defensive response.

The reason that behavioral accountability is more important than the quantitative, results-related kind has nothing to do with the fact that it is harder. It is due to the fact that behavioral problems almost always precede—and cause—a downturn in performance and results.

59

Whether we're talking about a football team, a sales department, or an elementary school, a meaningful drop in measurable performance can almost always be traced back to behavioral issues that made the drop possible. Lack of attention to details at practice, decreased discipline about cold-calling, poor preparation of lesson plans: all of these are behavioral problems that occur long before any decrease in measurable results is apparent. Great leaders and great team members confront one another about those behaviors early because they see the connection between the two and care enough about the team to take that risk before the results begin to suffer.

It's difficult to overstate the competitive advantage that an accountability-friendly organization has over one where leaders don't hold one another accountable. More than anything else, problems are identified and solved earlier and without the collateral damage of politics. Whether you measure that in terms of greater revenue, higher productivity, or reduced turnover, the benefits are massive and real.

It's worth pointing out here that people often confuse accountability with conflict because both involve discomfort and emotion. But there is an enormous difference between the two. Conflict is about issues and ideas, while accountability is about performance and behavior. As difficult as it is for many people to engage in conflict, at least it is somewhat objective, removed from a person's behavior. It is much harder for most people to hold one another accountable because it involves something of a personal, behavioral judgment.

Team Effectiveness Exercise

A good tool for teams that want to improve their ability to hold one another accountable is something we call the team effectiveness exercise. I'll explain it here in some detail because it's pretty simple, it requires only an hour or two, and it can transform how team members go about holding each other to higher standards of performance. It's just that powerful.

We usually do this exercise at the end of a two-day off-site meeting, but only when we believe the team has a decent foundation of trust (they usually do). If team members aren't capable of being vulnerable with one another, there is no point in doing it.

We start the exercise by having everyone write down one thing that each of the other team members does that makes the team better. In other words, they write down, for everyone other than themselves, the single biggest area of strength as it pertains to the impact on the group. We're interested not in their technical skills, but in the way they behave when the team is together that makes the team stronger.

Then we ask them to do the same thing, except this time focusing on the one aspect of each person that sometimes hurts the team. After ten or fifteen minutes of thoughtful consideration and note taking, everyone is usually done.

Then, starting with the leader, we go around the room asking everyone to report on the leader's one positive characteristic. We then allow the leader to provide his general, one-sentence reaction. In most cases, the leader is quite humbled by the positive feedback, sometimes even surprised by it. Then we go around the room again, asking people to report on the one characteristic that the leader needs to improve on. Again, we let the leader provide a brief reaction—not a rebuttal, but simply a reaction—to the feedback after everyone has provided their input. In virtually every case, there is acceptance and appreciation.

And then we do the same exercise for every other member of the team. It takes about ten minutes for each person to receive both the positive and constructive feedback from peers and to provide his or her simple reactions. After an hour or two, depending on the size of the team, the exercise is complete. It's usually at this point that people are sitting around the table in a state of mild amazement at the direct, honest, and helpful feedback that they've just shared.

The benefit of this exercise goes far beyond the mere sharing of information, as important as that is. The greatest impact is the realization on the part of leadership team members that holding one another accountable is a survivable and productive activity, and it will make them likely to continue doing it going forward. And in some situations, the eventual result is particularly powerful.

Voluntary Turnover

One of our consultants was working with the leadership team of a large company's information technology department. Many members of the team were struggling with the behavior of one of their peers, Fred, who had a close relationship with the CIO who was in charge of the team. They didn't believe that the CIO was holding Fred accountable for his destructive behavior, that he was playing favorites. The CIO would later admit that he valued Fred's technical expertise and was reluctant to do anything that might cause him to leave.

During an off-site meeting, the team confronted the CIO about his lack of consistent accountability across the team, in particular, with Fred. The CIO acknowledged the issue and announced that he would work on it.

Over the course of the following months, the CIO started to hold Fred more accountable. Just as important, the team followed suit, engaging with Fred more directly about his behavior. Without the protection that he had grown accustomed to getting from his boss, Fred eventually decided that he didn't want to be a part of the team, and he left the company.

Contrary to his fears about losing Fred, the CIO found that the performance of the rest of his team improved. He attributed that to Fred's absence and the new culture of accountability that the team had embraced.

Losing a team member is not at all a common outcome of building a culture of accountability. In most cases, team members simply learn to demand more of one another and watch their collective performance improve. In some cases, though, the only way for them to do that is by losing someone from the team. But again, that's certainly not the norm.

No matter what the situation, there will always be some discomfort as team members confront one another about their behavior. In the end, however, the level of cohesion and personal satisfaction among team members who embrace the new philosophy overwhelms any temporary discomfort.

Public Versus Private

I'm often asked whether leaders should hold their people accountable privately during one-on-one sessions or in more public forums with the whole team, like during meetings. Although every case is a little different, generally I believe that on cohesive teams, accountability is best handled with the entire team. I say this because when leaders and team members call one another on issues in front of team members, they get benefits that don't occur when it takes place individually.

First, when accountability is handled during a meeting, every member of the team receives the message simultaneously and doesn't have to make the same mistakes in order to learn the lesson of the person being held accountable. Second, they know that the leader is holding their colleague accountable, which avoids their wondering whether the boss is doing his job. Finally, it serves to reinforce the culture of accountability, which increases the likelihood that team members will do the same for one another. When leaders—and peers— limit their accountability discussions to private conversations, they leave people wondering whether those discussions are happening. This often leads to unproductive hallway conversations and conjecture about who knows what about whom.

Having said all that, when it comes to addressing relatively serious issues, or matters of corrective action in which a leader is wondering whether a member of the team might not be worthy to be on the team anymore, then everything changes. These are best handled privately, in a one-on-one situation, to respect the dignity of the person being held accountable. However, and this can be dicey, the leader is often well advised to let her people know that she is addressing the situation to avoid unproductive and dangerous speculation.

As uncomfortable and difficult as it can often be, accountability helps a team and an organization avoid far more costly and difficult situations later. It also allows a team to embrace the last behavior that is critical for a cohesive team: the focus on results.

BEHAVIOR 5: FOCUSING ON RESULTS

The ultimate point of building greater trust, conflict, commitment, and accountability is one thing: the achievement of results. That certainly seems obvious, but as it turns out, one of the greatest challenges to team success is the inattention to results. What would members of an executive team be focused on if not the results of their organization? Well, for one, the results of their department. Too many leaders seem to have a greater affinity for and loyalty to the department they lead rather than the team they're a member of and the organization they are supposed to be collectively serving. Other distractions include a concern for individual career development, budget allocations, status, and ego, all of them common distractions that prevent teams from being obsessed with achieving results.

Some people find this extreme emphasis on results to be a little cold and uninspiring. But there is no getting around the fact that the only measure of a great team—or a great organization—is whether it accomplishes what it sets out to accomplish. Some leaders of teams that don't regularly

> No matter how good a leadership team feels about itself, and how noble its mission might be, if the organization it leads rarely achieves its goals, then, by definition, it's simply not a good team.

succeed will still insist that they have a great team because team members care about one other and no one ever leaves the team. A more accurate description of their situation would be to say that they have a mediocre team that enjoys being together and isn't terribly bothered by failure. See, no matter how good a leadership team feels about itself, and how noble its mission might be, if the organization it leads rarely achieves its goals, then, by definition, it's simply not a good team.

Keep in mind that revenue and profitability are not the only measures of achievement, even in for-profit organizations (though they are certainly critical ones). The definition of results and achievement will vary from one organization to another depending on the reason that a given organization exists. A football team most likely will measure itself in terms of wins and losses, a school in terms of how well it prepares students for their next step in education, and a church based on how many parishioners are growing in their faith. That's not to say that all of those organizations will not have financial measurements; it's just that finances are probably not going to be their primary measure of results.

In traditional for-profit companies, financial metrics are certainly going to take a more prominent place in the hierarchy of goals, as they should. After all, they are the indicator of how well a company is serving its customers and fulfilling its mission. However, even in these organizations, other measures will often be just as important as, if not more important than, profit. Plenty of businesses, usually smaller, privately held ones, make decisions every day to do something for customers that may never benefit them financially. They do it because they think it's the right thing to do, or because they think it might eventually help them become more influential in the market. Regardless of their rationale, if they make that decision consciously, knowing what they want to achieve, then they are still focusing on results.

Collective Goals

When it comes to how a cohesive team measures its performance, one criterion sets it apart from noncohesive ones: its goals are shared across the entire team. This is not just a theoretical way of saying that people should help one another. It's far more specific, and far more difficult too.

In most organizations, results are compartmentalized by department. Executives see themselves as having little or no responsibility for goals that fall outside their functional areas of expertise. This, of course, is the antithesis of teamwork, though somehow it doesn't deter many leaders from calling themselves teams and preaching the importance of working together across functions.

The only way for a team to really be a team and to maximize its output is to ensure that everyone is focused on the same priorities—rowing in the same direction, if you will. When the marketing department defines itself by how well it does marketing and the other departments do the same in their functional areas, there is no reason to expect synergy within the team. As simple as that may sound, most leadership teams still do not seem to understand this.

One Team, One Score

After a recent loss, a thirteen-year-old boy on my son's soccer team said to me, "Well, I don't feel like I lost."

"Really?" I asked him. "How do you figure?"

He proudly announced, "Well, I'm a forward, and we forwards did our part by scoring three goals. It's really the defense that lost the game because they gave up too many goals. They're the losers."

I kindly pointed out to him how absurd his reasoning was, not only because there is only one score for the team, but because every player on the field plays defense, though perhaps on different parts of the field. Even a forward plays a role in preventing the other team from scoring by making it difficult for the opponent's defense to organize an attack.

To be fair, the kid smiled and acknowledged the ridiculousness of his original remark.

I wish I could say that it was that easy to convince leadership team members. Too many of them don't see a connection between the decisions they make and the impact they have on other parts of the business. They don't seem to understand that the way they spend their time, energy, and resources can influence the overall performance of the organization. All too often they embrace the attitude embodied by the fisherman who looks at the guy sitting at the other end of the boat and announces, "Hey, your side of the boat is sinking."

Great teams ensure that all members, in spite of their individual responsibilities and areas of expertise, are doing whatever they can to help the team accomplish its goals. That means they need to be asking difficult questions about what is happening in other departments and volunteering, in any way they can, to help those parts of the business that might be struggling and might jeopardize the success of the entire organization.

Team Number One

The only way for a leader to establish this collective mentality on a team is by ensuring that all members place a higher priority on the team they're a member of than the team they lead in their departments. A good way to go about this is simply to ask them which team is their first priority. I've found that many well-intentioned executives will admit that in spite of their commitment to the team that they're a member of, the team they lead is their first priority. They'll point out that they hired their direct reports, they sit near them and spend more time with them every day, and they enjoy being the leader of that team. Moreover, they feel a sense of loyalty to the people they manage, and feel that those people want and need their protection.

This is absolutely natural, common, and understandable. And dangerous.

When members of a leadership team feel a stronger sense of commitment and loyalty to the team they lead than the one they're a member of, then the team they're a member of becomes like the U.S. Congress or the United Nations: it's just a place where people come together to lobby for their constituents. Teams that lead healthy organizations reject this model and come to terms with the difficult but critical requirement that executives must put the needs of the higher team ahead of the needs of their departments. That is the only way that good decisions can be made about how best to serve the entire organization and maximize its performance.

> Teams that lead healthy organizations come to terms with the difficult but critical requirement that its members must put the needs of the higher team ahead of the needs of their departments.

The advantage that can be achieved by shifting a team's priorities from individual to collective ones, and thus demonstrating a true commitment to team number one, is undeniable.

First Team

We worked with the CIO of a massive corporation. She was struggling with team members who seemed to be working almost exclusively on their own priorities, with little concern for what was happening with their peers in other departments. As a result, there was minimal cooperation and synergy, and the overall performance and reputation of the IT organization had suffered.

Confronting the problem with the team, the CIO announced that they would be taking specific and difficult measures to refocus the staff on their team number one. Those steps included moving each of her direct reports away from their departments and onto the same floor in the same building of the company's sprawling campus. She would also pull the team together every morning for a five-minute informal gathering to begin building the kind of professional and personal relationships that would be necessary to turn the organization around and thus better serve the company.

At first, her direct reports resisted. They didn't want to leave the physical and emotional comfort of their departments and were concerned that their own direct reports would feel abandoned as a result. But because she was their boss, they complied.

Within just a few months, the behavior of the executives, the synergy within the team, and the overall performance of the organization had improved dramatically. "Somehow we became a new team with a collective focus, instead of a bunch of subdepartments doing their own thing. We can't imagine going back to the old way," remarked one of the CIO's reports. "And even the people in my department benefited when they saw how aligned and focused we had become as leaders."

The surprising power of embracing team number one is one of the most gratifying and powerful things we witness in the work we do with leaders.

Testament to Unity

One of our consultants was working with the CEO of a mental health hospital who was tired of his staff members' pursuing their own agendas. Over a period of a few months, the two of them worked to shift the team's focus to the collective good of the organization.

The CEO's reaction to what happened says it all: "The concept of team number one has created a common language and sense of identity for our team. It provides the mind-set that individual goals, issues, and interests are set aside to focus on what's best for the organization. I truly believe it is the one thing that keeps us from busting apart at the seams as we deal with the challenging issues of managing in a complex business environment."

CHECKLIST FOR DISCIPLINE 1:
BUILD A COHESIVE LEADERSHIP TEAM

Members of a leadership team can be confident that they've mastered this discipline when they can affirm the following statements:

— The leadership team is small enough (three to ten people) to be effective.

— Members of the team trust one another and can be genuinely vulnerable with each other.

— Team members regularly engage in productive, unfiltered conflict around important issues.

— The team leaves meetings with clear-cut, active, and specific agreements around decisions.

— Team members hold one another accountable to commitments and behaviors.

— Members of the leadership team are focused on team number one. They put the collective priorities and needs of the larger organization ahead of their own departments.

WHAT'S IT WORTH TO YOU?

Again, let's imagine two different organizations.

The first is led by a team whose members share a common passion for what they do and are committed to abiding by the same set of values. They have a clear plan for success and know exactly how they differ from their competition. At any given moment, they can articulate their top, collective priority, and they understand how every member of the team contributes to achieving that priority.

The second is run by a group of well-intentioned executives who have a good understanding of the details of their business. But they don't spend much time thinking or talking about why their organization exists or what values should drive their behaviors. Though they talk about being more strategic, they can't really articulate a simple, clear strategy, and they don't have a consistent method for evaluating decisions. The leadership team is constantly managing against a long list of eclectic goals, some of which may not be compatible and most of which pertain to only a few members of the team. Moreover, most team members have somewhat limited knowledge about and interest in the specific responsibilities of their peers.

The question: What kind of advantage would the first organization have over the second, and how much time and energy would it be worth investing to make this advantage a reality?

Create Clarity

The second requirement for building a healthy organization—creating clarity—is all about achieving alignment. This is a word that is used incessantly by leaders, consultants, and organizational theorists, and yet for all the attention it gets, real alignment remains frustratingly rare. Most executives who run organizations—and certainly the employees who work for them—will readily attest to this.

A big part of the reason for the failure to gain alignment has to do with the fact that, like so many other popular terms, people use it without being specific about what they mean. Within the context of making an organization healthy, alignment is about creating so much clarity that there is as little room as possible for confusion, disorder, and infighting

73

to set in. Of course, the responsibility for creating that clarity lies squarely with the leadership team.

Unfortunately, most of the leaders I've worked with who complain about a lack of alignment mistakenly see it primarily as a behavioral or attitudinal problem. In their minds, it's a function of the fact that employees below them do not want to work together. What those executives don't realize is that there cannot be alignment deeper in the organization, even when employees want to cooperate, if the leaders at the top aren't in lockstep with one another around a few very specific things.

> All too often leaders underestimate the impact of even subtle misalignment at the top and the damage caused by small gaps among members of the executive team.

Of course, few executives will dispute this. It's hard to argue with the idea that egregious and fundamental differences among leadership team members create obstacles to alignment and success. But all too often —and this is critical— leaders underestimate the impact of even subtle misalignment at the top, and the damage caused to the rest of the organization by small gaps among members of the executive team.

Thinking they're being mature, leaders often agree to disagree with one another around seemingly minor issues, thereby avoiding what they see as unnecessary contentiousness and conflict. After all, from their vantage point, the gaps in their opinions and decisions seem small and innocuous. What they don't understand is that by failing to eliminate even those small gaps, they are leaving employees below them to fight bloody, unwinnable battles with their peers in other departments. This leads to the antithesis of (oh, I hate to use this word) empowerment.

No matter how many times executives preach about the "e" word in their speeches, there is no way that their employees can be empowered to fully execute their responsibilities if they don't receive clear and consistent messages about what is important from their leaders across the organization. There is probably no greater frustration for employees than having to constantly navigate the politics and confusion caused by leaders who are misaligned. That's because just a little daylight between members of a leadership team becomes blinding and overwhelming to employees one or two levels below. I've heard this referred to as the "vortex effect." Whatever you call it, it's real, it's a big problem, and it makes deep organizational alignment impossible.

Okay, assuming that there is agreement around the benefits of clarity and alignment, the next logical question would be, *How do we go about achieving it?* Before answering that question, I think it might be helpful to take a look at an example of how not to do it.

BLATHER

Since the 1980s, many organizations have centered their clarity and alignment efforts around a singular tool that has been a major disappointment. What I'm referring to is the mission statement.

Though I can't be sure, I suspect that at some point about thirty years ago a cleverly sadistic and antibusiness consultant decided that the best way to really screw up companies was to convince them that what they needed was a convoluted, jargony, and all-encompassing declaration of intent. The more times those declarations used phrases like "world class," "shareholder value," and "adding value," the better. And if companies would actually print those declarations and hang them in their lobbies and break rooms for public viewing, well, that would be a real coup.

Even if my historical suspicions are untrue, it can't be denied that most mission statements have neither inspired people to change the world nor provided them with an accurate description of what an organization actually does for a living. They certainly haven't created alignment and clarity among employees. What they have done is make many leadership teams look foolish.

Just in case you're not convinced of this, take a look at the following mission statement I've lifted from the T-shirt of a company that most people know fairly well. I've redacted the name of the organization and just one word that might give away its industry. See if you can guess which company it is.

MISSION STATEMENT

_____ Incorporated provides its customers with quality _____ products and the expertise required for making informed buying decisions. We provide our products and services with a dedication to the highest degree of integrity and quality of customer satisfaction, developing long-term professional relationships with employees that develop pride, creating a stable working environment and company spirit.

As bad as it is, it's hard to deny that this statement seems fairly ordinary, like so many others that we've come across in our careers. And yet what makes this one particularly noteworthy is that it is meant to be a joke. You see, this is the mission statement of Dunder Mifflin, the fictional paper company featured on the timeless sitcom, *The Office.*

> Alignment and clarity cannot be achieved in one fell swoop with a series of buzzwords and aspirational phrases crammed together. It requires a much more rigorous and unpretentious approach.

That's right. It's a spoof. And yet it sounds like so many of the mission statements we've seen hanging in the lobbies of companies where we do business.

The point here is that alignment and clarity cannot be achieved in one fell swoop with a series of generic buzzwords and aspirational phrases crammed together. Leaders simply cannot inspire, inform, motivate, market, and position their companies in the context of a T-shirt or Lucite tchotchke. Clarity requires a much more rigorous and unpretentious approach.

SIX CRITICAL QUESTIONS

What leaders must do to give employees the clarity they need is agree on the answers to six simple but critical questions and thereby eliminate even small discrepancies in their thinking. None of these questions is novel per se. What is new is the realization that none of them can be addressed in isolation; they must be answered together. Failing to achieve alignment around any one of them can prevent an organization from attaining the level of clarity necessary to become healthy.

These are the six questions:

1. Why do we exist?
2. How do we behave?
3. What do we do?
4. How will we succeed?
5. What is most important, right now?
6. Who must do what?

If members of a leadership team can rally around clear answers to these fundamental questions — without using jargon and smarmy language—they will drastically increase the likelihood of creating a healthy organization. This may well be the most important step of all in achieving the advantage of organizational health.

Answering these questions, like everything else in this book, is as difficult as it is theoretically simple. It's simple in that it doesn't require great intellectual capacity or cleverness; every leadership team has more than enough information and experience to achieve clarity. It can be difficult, however, for a variety of reasons.

First, as we explored in the last chapter, it requires cohesion at the top. A team that isn't behaviorally cohesive won't be able to engage in the level of passionate, messy dialogue that is required to achieve real buy-in around these questions.

Second—and this is a big one—it's often tempting for leaders to slip into a marketing or sloganizing mind-set when answering these questions, trying to come up with catchy phrases or impressive-sounding statements. This is a sign that the team is missing the boat and has been distracted from its real purpose: establishing true clarity and alignment.

Finally, answering these questions requires time. Not months, but certainly a few days up front followed by a little more time in the following weeks to fully bake the answers. Taking time to sit with the questions and ensure that all members of the leadership team understand what they mean and are truly aligned around the answers is essential.

But what if the answers they come up with are wrong? Here's the thing: there are no right or wrong answers. I mean, who's to say what is right and wrong when it comes to setting the direction of an organization? After all, there's more than one way to skin a cat, or so I've been told. More than getting the *right* answer, it is important to simply have *an* answer—one that is directionally correct and around which all team members can commit.

> More than getting the *right* answer, it's often more important to simply have *an* answer—one that is directionally correct and around which all team members can commit.

78

PERFECTION PARALYSIS

So many organizations struggle with this idea that there are no right answers. I think they've been influenced by academics, analysts, and industry pundits who falsely attribute business success to intellectual precision and accuracy in decision making. The stories journalists write always seem to conclude that a company succeeded because it came up with the right strategic answers, even though the leaders of those organizations will almost always tell you that what they were really good at was not necessarily having the right answer, but rather being able to rally around the best answer they could find at the time. This tendency to apply twenty-twenty hindsight to success falsely leads people to think that intelligence and precision, rather than clarity, are key.

Plenty of euphemisms attest to this idea that implementation science is more important than decision science. One I heard years ago comes from the military: *a* plan is better than *no* plan. And it was General Patton who once said, "A good plan violently executed today is better than a perfect plan executed next week." Those adages attest to something I've seen among too many leadership teams: a simple failure to achieve clarity because executives are waiting for perfection. In the meantime, confusion reigns, leaders lose credibility, and the organization suffers.

Wait for It . . .

The head of marketing for a large company I once worked for complained incessantly about the CEO's lack of decisiveness. "When is this guy going to announce a strategic direction for the company?" was his mantra-like rhetorical question. He was relentless, and to be fair, many of us agreed with him even if we didn't like his dismissive attitude toward his boss.

Well, the board finally removed the CEO and, wouldn't you know it, put the head of marketing in charge of the company. Though we liked the previous chief executive, we were excited by the prospect that the organization now had a leader who was finally going to declare a position in the market and chart a course for the future.

For the first few weeks of the new CEO's tenure, we gently asked him if he was ready to communicate the company's new direction.

"Not yet," he assured us. "I'm waiting for a few things to take shape first."

That seemed reasonable for a new leader, so we decided to give him time. But for the next few months, he kept putting us off. "The market is changing," he would say as we encouraged him to set the course for the company. Meanwhile, employees grumbled, competitors outflanked us, and paralysis set in, all because the leader wanted to find the perfect plan.

Nine months later—I promise that this actually happened—we were still operating without a clear statement of direction. The only thing the CEO was willing to commit to, in terms of anything new regarding clarity, was a three-word slogan to be used for marketing purposes (and yes, the three words rhymed).

Of course, that's not to say that leaders should just come up with any answer to these questions without regard to whether or not they are directionally correct. That would be ridiculous. It's just to say that waiting for clear confirmation that a decision is exactly right is a recipe for mediocrity and almost a guarantee of eventual failure. That's because organizations learn by making decisions, even bad ones. By being decisive, leaders allow themselves to get clear, immediate data from their actions. As a result, they are often able to change course and defeat their indecisive competitors who, while congratulating themselves for not making a mistake, are too mired in theoretical analysis paralysis to rally around any clear plan.

Now that we've acknowledged the danger of seeking perfection at the expense of decisiveness, let's take on each of the six critical questions that leaders must answer in order to create clarity and build a healthy organization.

QUESTION 1: WHY DO WE EXIST?

Answering this question requires a leadership team to identify its underlying reason for being, also known as its core purpose. Jim Collins and Jerry Porras introduced the idea of core purpose in their great book, *Built to Last*.[1] They asserted that successful, enduring organizations understand the fundamental reason they were founded and why they exist, and they stay true to that reason. This helps them avoid losing their way.

I certainly believe that Collins and Porras were right. Unfortunately, too many of the teams I've come across in my consulting work fail to properly capture what the authors intended. Instead, they end up with uninspiring and mediocre mission statements that are neither lofty enough nor descriptive enough to be helpful (see the Dunder Mifflin example in the previous "Blather" section).

> Employees in every organization, and at every level, need to know that at the heart of what they do lies something grand and aspirational.

An organization's core purpose—why it exists—has to be completely idealistic. I can't reiterate this point enough. Many leadership teams struggle with this, afraid that what they come up with will seem too grand or aspirational. Of course, that's the whole point. Employees in every organization, and at every level, need to know that at the heart of what they do lies something grand and aspirational. They're well aware that ultimately it will boil down to tangible, tactical activities.

In order to successfully identify their organization's purpose, leaders must accept the notion that all organizations exist to make people's lives better. Again, that sounds idealistic, but every enterprise—every last one—ultimately should exist to do just that. To aspire to anything less would be foolish. After all, no one doubts that every company must have some sort of value proposition—a compelling reason that customers or constituents want to interact with it. And at the heart of that interaction is the expectation of a better life.

Now that doesn't mean that all organizations make people's lives better in major, transformational ways. Most do so in relatively small, subtle ways. And it doesn't mean that they make *all* people's lives better; usually it's a relatively small subset of the population. Nonetheless, every organization must contribute in some way to a better world for some group of people, because if it doesn't, it will, and should, go out of business.

Assuming that a given organization does, in fact, have the potential for identifying an underlying reason for being—I've yet to meet one that doesn't—the challenge then is to identify and articulate that reason. If leaders can't do that, they cannot rightfully expect employees to get out of bed every morning with any sense of purpose beyond completing tasks and keeping their jobs.

There is a darn good chance that your company—in fact, any given company—has not yet identified its purpose. I've found that most have not, at least not adequately. And I've come to realize that even organizations that think they have usually haven't done so with the degree of rigor and specificity that is necessary. This leads to two problems.

First, those teams don't achieve a real sense of collective commitment from their members. Too often busy executives who want nothing to do with what they see as ethereal, metaphysical conversations simply nod their heads and agree with whatever the team comes up with for a statement of purpose. This is a recipe for jargony, empty declarations.

Second, and this is certainly related, those executives don't see the company's reason for existing as having any practical implications for the way they make decisions and run the organization. As a result of having no real idealistic boundaries, they operate in a largely reactive, shortsighted way, being overly tactical and opportunistic. And they often lose their way by getting involved in a variety of random pursuits and projects that might be financially justifiable in the short term but don't really fit together. This tends to dilute the focus and passion that employees look for when they're coming to work.

Some executives, especially those who are a little cynical about all this purpose stuff, will say that their company exists simply *to make money for owners or shareholders.* That is almost never a purpose, but rather an important indicator of success. It's how an organization knows that it is effectively fulfilling its purpose, but it falls far short of providing the organization with a guide to what ultimately matters most.

In those rare companies where business owners really do believe that the organization's underlying purpose is to provide themselves with financial windfalls, it is best that leaders are up front about that purpose. Otherwise they'll create confusion, cynicism, and a sense of betrayal among employees who almost always prefer a more idealistic reason for coming to work.

Finding Your Reason for Existing

When leaders set about identifying the purpose of their organization, there are a few critical factors they must keep in mind to give them a good chance at success.

First, they must be clear that answering this question is not the end of the clarity process. They will have the opportunity, in short order, to clarify more tactical areas of focus for the organization in a less idealistic, more practical way. Knowing this gives them the confidence they need to be purely idealistic in their momentary pursuit of addressing this question and to avoid the guilt-driven temptation to include too many practical concepts that are of a more tactical nature.

Second, an organization's reason for existence, its purpose, has to be true. It must be based on the real motivations of the people who founded or are running the organization, not something that simply sounds good on paper. Identifying an organization's true purpose becomes difficult when that organization has been around for a long time, sometimes for decades, and has never really clarified its underlying reason for being. In those cases, leaders have to go back and try to understand why its founders started the organization or, at the very least, to connect their current motivations to the organization's history. If this isn't doable, then those leaders need to go about this process as though they were rebirthing the company themselves, and they must be prepared to stick with their answer for as long as the organization exists.

Third, the process of determining an organization's purpose cannot be confused with marketing, external or internal. It must be all about clarity and alignment. Certainly it will be important to eventually communicate the answer to the entire organization, and maybe even to integrate it into external communication when appropriate. But a real danger, and a common one, occurs when leaders confuse their motivation for identifying their purpose with trying to come up with something that will sound impressive on a billboard, in an annual report, or on an employee sweatshirt.

When leaders do this, confusing marketing with creating clarity, they often commit the subsequent error of making a big, formal announcement about the company's purpose. This only provokes cynicism. I try to remind them that even if they never wrote it down or formally communicated their core purpose (not that I would ever recommend this), if it lived only in the hearts and minds of the leadership team, it could still do its job by guiding their decisions and actions and keeping the company grounded. Eventually it would become apparent to employees and customers alike, even without billboards and sweatshirts.

So how does an organization go about figuring out why it exists? It starts by asking this question: "How do we contribute to a better world?" Again, skeptics who think this sounds soft or ethereal need to remember that this is not the end of the clarity process and that it is critical to create a framework for more tactical decisions.

Usually the first answer that leaders come up with is not ideal enough—for example: *We help companies use technology to do more business with their partners. We pave driveways so people can get in and out of their houses and go places. We teach kids how to do their homework better.*

Those are a start, but they're certainly not lofty enough. As Porras and Collins say, the next question that needs to be asked, and asked again and again until it leads to the highest purpose or reason for existence, is *Why? Why do we do that? Why do we help companies use technology to do more business with their partners? Why do we pave driveways? Why do we teach kids how to do their homework better?*

Eventually, by answering that question again and again, a leadership team will get to a point where they've identified the most idealistic reason for their business. That point will be somewhere just shy of *to make the world a better place.* That's how they'll know they're done.

"Why Do We Exist?" Categories

A tricky part of this is understanding that there are a number of very different categories of purpose, any of which can be valid. Identifying which category fits your organization's purpose can be very helpful in focusing your discussion of why your organization exists because it better clarifies who the organization ultimately serves.

Customer: This purpose is directly related to serving the needs of an organization's customer or primary constituent. For instance, a hotel might exist simply because its founder always believed in serving customers. In other words, it's about pleasing the human beings who walk through its doors. How does that inform the leaders? Well, if customers have a need, the hotel should try to fill it, because that would be true to its purpose. And the hotel shouldn't hire people who don't love to serve customers.

The department store Nordstrom is a good example of this. Their underlying motivation for everything they do is about serving custom-

86

ers. Period. It's not really about fashion, though they certainly need to be good at that; it's about giving people what they're looking for, no matter what.

Industry: This purpose is all about being immersed in a given industry. Getting back to the hotel example, maybe it exists because its owners just love the hotel business. It isn't going to try to get into other lines of business that are not central to hotels, and it isn't going to hire people who don't think that hotels are cool.

Many smaller businesses and entrepreneurial ventures fall into this category: they simply love the nature of their industry. That's why its founders started their business in the first place: to do what they love.

One that comes to mind is a horse-training company one of our consultants has worked with in Texas. The founder and CEO grew up on a ranch in Australia and loves everything to do with horses. So his stated purpose is "to inspire the dreams of horsemen." Everything his company does is born out of a love for horses and the people who share that love.

Greater Cause: This kind of purpose is not necessarily about what the organization does, but about something connected to it. For instance, a hotel might exist because its owner is a fanatic about vacations. Or maybe it's all about allowing people to experience luxury. Or the importance of special occasions. It's not about hotels per se, and it's not simply about making any customer happy. The hotel exists because it believes in something that a hotel can play a role in making a reality. Ideally employees ought to buy into, if not share, a passion for vacations, luxury, celebrating special occasions, or whatever else it is that drives the owners or leaders of the organization.

The reason that Southwest Airlines exists is to democratize air travel in America. It believes that flying on airplanes shouldn't be reserved for the wealthy and that all people should be able to attend a family reunion, go on vacation, or do business with clients in another city without sacrificing their financial security. That's why the airline was started. Does it serve customers? Sure. Do they enjoy aviation? Yeah. But those are not the fundamental reasons that Southwest is in business. Its leaders have a larger cause associated with that service, and that cause informs every decision they make. For instance, they are committed to low prices. To violate that commitment would be to violate their purpose because democratizing travel can't happen if large numbers of customers are priced out of the market.

Community: This purpose is about doing something that makes a specific geographical place better. For instance, our fictional hotel might exist simply to provide a city or region with a nice place for visitors, events, or business. It's about pride in a community. The hotel will do whatever else it can to contribute to that community, and employees who share a love for and commitment to the area will thrive there.

The head of a youth soccer club near my office told me that his underlying purpose is not really about soccer itself (of course, he loves soccer too), but about serving his local town. He grew up in that community and returned there to run the club even though there are other clubs with more money and better facilities nearby. His commitment to the community is why he insists on drawing mostly local talent and partnering with civic groups. And yes, like the neighboring clubs, he wants to win. But that's akin to a company wanting to make money: it's an indication of success, not the underlying reason for existing.

Employees: This purpose is not about serving the customer, the industry, or the region, but rather about the employees. Our fictional hotel might be all about giving employees a great work experience or providing a place to work for low-income people in the area. It will not make decisions or hire people who will jeopardize the well-being of employees.

A paving company I worked with struggled with identifying its fundamental purpose. After coming up with a few uninspiring ideas having to do with keeping driveways safe and making it possible for people to park their vehicles, the CEO/founder finally had an epiphany. He announced to his somewhat surprised executive team that his initial reason for starting the business had nothing to do with paving, but was really about helping poor, first-generation Americans find good jobs so they could buy their first homes and send their kids to college. To make his point clear, he explained that if the paving market tanked, he'd be fine going into roofing, or painting, or whatever other business would allow him to keep his employees working and their families moving forward in their lives.

Wealth: This purpose is about wealth for the owners. It's possible that our hotel exists simply because the person who owns it thinks it's a good way to make money for himself and his co-owners. This will and should inform the decisions that they make, with everything seen through a financial lens.

We don't run across many companies in this category (they probably don't come to us for help), although a number of venture capitalists and law firms we've seen would probably fit. Ultimately they aren't going to do anything that will reduce their near-term earnings potential or financial return, and they see customers, clients, and employees simply as a means to achieving that. If this is the real reason for existing, it's important for leaders to be clear about it, with themselves and the people who work for them. Otherwise they're going to waste a lot of time doing meaningless exercises and having fruitless conversations that only create confusion and cynicism among employees who are best served by knowing the clear truth.

Not a Differentiator

As we can see by using the example of the hotel, two companies that are in the same industry will often have different reasons for existing. That makes sense. However, it's also interesting to understand that two companies in completely different industries can share the same purpose. For instance, both a hospital and a masseuse could very well exist *to alleviate pain and suffering in the world*. Or a gardener and an artist might exist *to help people appreciate beauty*.

The point here is that an organization's reason for existing is not meant to be a differentiator and that the purpose for identifying it is only to clarify what is true in order to guide the business. When leaders try to use their purpose as a strategic differentiator, they usually fail to fully tap into the real reason for having one, and then find themselves disappointed when they learn that another company, perhaps even within their industry, shares theirs. They need to remember that it is simply about getting clarity.

It's important to keep in mind that the process of identifying why an organization exists is often a messy one. Because it's more of an art than a science, it's going to require a little time and plenty of fluid, unstructured discussion. And that's okay. The goal is not to get to an answer in the shortest amount of time possible, but rather to untap the true reason for the organization's existence. Of course leaders need to remember that it is only the first of six elements of organizational clarity.

QUESTION 2: HOW DO WE BEHAVE?

The word *intolerance* isn't often used in a positive way in society. And yet when it comes to creating organizational clarity and alignment, intolerance is essential. After all, if an organization is tolerant of everything, it will stand for nothing.

> If an organization is tolerant of everything, it will stand for nothing.

The answer to the question, *How do we behave?*, is embodied in an organization's core values, which should provide the ultimate guide for employee behavior at all levels. This too is an area that Collins and Porras addressed in *Built to Last*. In their research, they found that enduring, successful companies adhered strictly to a fundamental set of principles that guided their behaviors and decisions over time, preserving the essence of the organization.

The importance of values in creating clarity and enabling a company to become healthy cannot be overstated. More than anything else, values are critical because they define a company's personality. They provide employees with clarity about how to behave, which reduces the need for inefficient and demoralizing micromanagement.

That alone makes values worthwhile. But beyond that, an organization that has properly identified its values and adheres to them will naturally attract the right employees and repel the wrong ones. This makes recruiting exponentially easier and more effective, and it drastically reduces turnover.

The impact of values goes beyond employees. Clear values can also serve to attract and repel the right customers who want to do business with an organization that reflects what they value, and not just in some cause-related, theoretical sense. People who value creativity, for instance, often choose an organization that builds its culture around creativity.

Often this is a more effective means of marketing than expensive and easy-to-ignore programs around advertising, PR, and lead generation. Companies that are serious about their values find that the right customers eventually start to seek them out naturally.

Values Stampede

Collins and Porras made such a compelling case in their book that they set off a stampede of executives determined to find some core values of their own. Unfortunately, many of those executives missed the authors' point and came home from their off-site meetings with a long list of generic and uninspiring words that they then plastered onto posters, T-shirts, and Web sites. All too often, the result was an organization full of confused, frustrated, and cynical employees (and sometimes customers too).

The mistake those leaders made was trying to be all things to all people, which led them to make their values statements as broad and inclusive as possible. In many cases, this comes about because leaders conduct a survey asking employees to vote on which values they want, and then they try to accommodate all of the input they receive. Let me be very clear: this is a terrible process for identifying core values, for reasons that will become obvious later in this section.

When an organization announces that it has nine core values including customer service, innovation, quality, honesty, integrity, environmental responsibility, work-life balance, financial responsibility, and respect for the individual, it makes it impossible to use those values to make decisions, hire employees, or enact policies. After all, no action, person, or policy can meet all of those criteria.

This creates its own set of problems. When leaders who adopt too many values finally realize what they've done and that there is no hope for actually putting their many values to practical use, they often end up ignoring them altogether. In their heart of hearts, they come to see their value statement as a piece of internal marketing, even propaganda.

So they resign themselves to operating their companies in a pragmatic, valueless way, leaving employees and customers unsure of what the organization really stands for. When employees complain that the company's values are being violated, leaders just shrug their shoulders and focus on something more tangible.

Different Kinds of Values

An important key to identifying the right, small set of behavioral values is understanding that there are different kinds of values (something I wrote about a number of years ago in the *Harvard Business Review*).[2] Among these, core values are by far the most important and must not be confused with the others. Let's define the different types now so we don't get them confused:

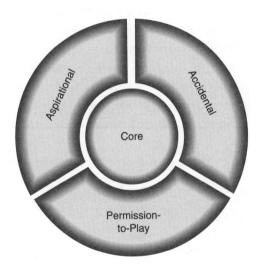

Core Values

These are the few—just two or three—behavioral traits that are inherent in an organization. Core values lie at the heart of the organization's identity, do not change over time, and must already exist. In other words, they cannot be contrived.

An organization knows that it has identified its core values correctly when it will allow itself to be punished for living those values and when it accepts the fact that employees will sometimes take those values too far. Core values are not a matter of convenience. They cannot be extracted from an organization any more than a human being's conscience can be extracted from his or her person. As a result, they should be used to guide every aspect of an organization, from hiring and firing to strategy and performance management.

Not for Everyone

We worked with an airline that is fanatical about its culture. It had three core values, one of which had to do with humor.

What testifies to the fact that this is a true core value is that the company refuses to hire people in any job, at any level, who don't have a sense of humor about themselves as well as life. Its leaders even go so far as to encourage and defend the humorous behaviors of their employees on the rare occasion when a customer doesn't appreciate it.

A great example of this occurred when a frequent flyer wrote to the company's CEO complaining that a flight attendant was making jokes during the preflight safety check. She was upset that the employee was trying to be funny while he was talking about something as serious and important as safety.

Now, most CEOs would respond to that complaint by thanking the customer for her time and her loyalty to the airline and assuring her that safety was, indeed, important to the organization. They would then promise to look into the matter to make sure that the flight attendant adjusts his behavior to avoid offending any other passengers who could be uncomfortable with the jokes. That would be reasonable enough, I suppose, unless your core values have to do with humor.

Well, the CEO of this company took a different approach. Rather than apologizing to the customer and asking the flight attendant to moderate his behavior, he wrote her a short note with three words on it: "We'll miss you." There can be little doubt that the company believed that humor was a core value.

(Rest assured that this company, like all good airlines, takes safety very, very seriously.)

Aspirational Values

These are the characteristics that an organization wants to have, wishes it already had, and believes it must develop in order to maximize its success in its current market environment. Aspirational values are the qualities that an organization is aspiring to adopt and will do its best to manage intentionally into the organization. However, they are neither natural nor inherent, which is why they must be purposefully inserted into the culture. But they should not be confused with core values, which, again, do not change over time and do not come and go with the needs of the business.

Wishful Thinking

I once worked with a CEO to identify the core values of his company. When I asked him what he thought one of the values might be, without hesitation he said "sense of urgency." I was a little surprised because the limited exposure I'd had with the employees at the company didn't mesh with that description. When I asked him if he believed that urgency was evident in the organization, he responded

"Heck no. We're complacent as hell. That's why it needs to be a core value."

What we advised that client to do was make "sense of urgency" an aspirational value and do everything it could to intentionally instill it in the organization. But they needed to avoid falsely claiming it as a core value, because that would only incite cynicism among employees who knew better.

Confusing core and aspirational values is a frequent mistake that companies make. It is critical that leaders understand the difference.

Aspirations

A small consulting firm I know was founded on the values of humility and passion. Every potential new hire had to pass the screening for those values, and every decision the firm made was scrutinized, to a certain extent, against whether it reflected humility and passion.

As the firm started to experience increased demand for its services, it realized that its informal, scrappy approach to serving clients wasn't scalable and needed to change. Essentially, it needed to instill a greater sense of professionalism and systematization in its operations.

Knowing that this was not inherent in its passionate, entrepreneurial culture, the founders decided to make "professionalism" one of the firm's aspirational values. That meant they would intentionally hire someone who had experience building a more mature and organized consulting practice. Of course, that person would have to embody the firm's core values too, because, as the president said, "To hire someone who wasn't humble and passionate would be like selling our soul."

The firm hired a new VP who met the core values criteria and brought a new level of professionalism to the firm. But they were careful to remind themselves that this was not something that came naturally to them and that they would always have to work at it so that the firm could continue growing.

Permission-to-Play Values

These values are the minimum behavioral standards that are required in an organization. Although they are extremely important, permission-to-play values don't serve to clearly define or differentiate an organization from others. Values that commonly fit into this category include honesty, integrity, and respect for others. If those sound generic, something you've seen on virtually all of the values statements plastered on the walls of every mediocre company you've ever visited, then you understand the problem. Permission-to-play values must be delineated from the core to avoid dilution and genericism (I don't think that's a word, but you get the point).

Integrity About Integrity

An executive team at a technology start-up we worked with insisted that integrity was a core value of their company (many of our clients do this).

They justified this by explaining that they would never hire someone who lied during an interview or put false information on a résumé. We explained that most organizations had similar policies and that unless they were willing to adopt clearly higher standards for integrity than most other companies, and then stand by those standards even in the face of serious market pressure, they should classify integrity as a permission-to-play value.

They initially refused, saying, "But if we don't have integrity as one of our core values, then people will think we don't care about it."

During a subsequent meeting, executives discussed the possibility of doing some competitive intelligence gathering in a manner that could easily appear to be unethical to some people. We reminded them about their insistence on including integrity as a core value. They relented and reclassified it as permission-to-play.

Accidental Values

These values are the traits that are evident in an organization but have come about unintentionally and don't necessarily serve the good of the organization. In many companies, behavioral tendencies develop over time because of history, or because people start to hire employees who come from similar backgrounds. One day everyone looks around and realizes that just about every employee who works in the organization shares some quality: socioeconomic status, introversion, or good looks. The question that needs to be asked is whether being middle class, introverted, or good looking is something that the company has cultivated for a purpose, or whether it came about accidentally. It's important that leaders guard against accidental values taking root because they can prevent new ideas and people from flourishing in an organization. Sometimes they even sabotage its success by shutting out new perspectives and even potential customers.

Unintended Consequences

A fashion accessory company we worked with during its founding adopted a strong set of three core values that it carefully built its operations around.

A few years later, we visited the company's headquarters after not having seen them for quite some time. They had grown considerably and had hired dozens of new employees. But something struck me about the new hires: they all seemed to be in their early twenties and were wearing the same kind of mod, hip, black clothes.

I asked the CEO, "When did you adopt a new core value?"

He seemed confused, so I pointed out that the company seemed to be hiring people who fit a common demographic and stylistic profile. It was only then that he realized that they had accidentally adopted a certain youthful, hip culture, one that had nothing to do with their customer base and that could potentially limit the appeal of their company to prospective candidates. They took steps to revisit their hiring methods and their decision making.

Isolating the Core

The key to sifting core values from the others, especially aspirational and permission-to-play values, is to ask a few difficult questions. For instance, separating core from aspirational values can be done by asking the questions, *Is this trait inherent and natural for us, and has it been apparent in the organization for a long time? Or, is it something that we have to work hard to cultivate?* A core value will have been apparent for a long time and requires little intentional provocation.

Permission-to-play values are also often confused with core. The best way to differentiate them is to ask, *Would our organization be able to credibly claim that we are more committed to this value than 99 percent of the companies in our industry?* If so, then maybe it really is core. If not, then it's probably a candidate for permission-to-play; it's still important and should be used as a filter in hiring, but it's not what sets the organization apart and uniquely defines it.

It's worth restating that the reason organizations need to understand the various kinds of values is to prevent them from getting confused with and diluting the core. Core values are what matters most.

Choosing a Name

Another key to successfully undertaking the core value process is deciding what to call a core value once you've identified it. The key is to avoid excessive wordsmithing while at the same time finding the most descriptive and effective phrase. I find it helpful for leaders to choose a unique, nontraditional word or phrase—something that doesn't already have such a worn legacy in society that everyone assumes they know what it means. Of course, once a name or a term has been chosen, it will be important for the leadership team to define that term with the most vivid and behavioral description possible. And the best way to do that is to write a description of what that value looks like in action.

Floor Sweeper

One start-up client I worked with described one of its core values as "willing to sweep floors." Most companies would have described it simply as "hard work," and few people outside the organization knew exactly what it meant. But that was a good thing because it gave the company the opportunity to define the phrase in its own way.

In their case, the leaders described "willing to sweep floors" as having no concerns about status and ego and willing to do whatever was necessary to help the company succeed. No job was beneath any employee, and even the highest-level executive had to be willing to do the most menial work if that's what was needed.

The value was so powerful that the day after the leadership team established it, one of its members decided to quit because he just didn't see himself as being a floor sweeper. Without bitterness, he acknowledged that he had an ego and that a big part of his career was building a résumé. He didn't want to hold the team back by being a misfit.

The CEO gladly accepted his resignation with no hard feelings, relieved to have addressed the cultural discrepancy before it became a bigger problem. A few years later, the executive who left the start-up called our consulting firm to have us work with his new company. He appreciated the clarity that we had helped the start-up achieve and wanted to build a similarly clear and strong culture in his new firm.

The problem for organizations that choose common words like *innovation* or *quality* is that everyone has their own understanding of those terms. That makes it a little more difficult for leaders to establish their own definition. Of course, none of this matters if the values that an organization adopts are not real ones. When leaders choose elaborate and unique phrases for their values but don't adhere to them, they generate more cynicism and distrust than if they said nothing at all.

Once an organization successfully identifies and describes its core values and separates them from the other kinds, it must then do its best to be intolerant of violations of those values. It must ensure that every activity it undertakes, every employee it hires, and every policy it enacts reflects those core values. Few organizations actually take this important step, instead allowing their values to be minimized as mere idealism rather than real building blocks of operations and culture. For those who are serious about their values, this is why it's so important not to dilute the power of core values or nullify it altogether by having too many. Later in the book, when I discuss reinforcing clarity, I'll get into the various ways that healthy organizations can build their values into their processes that revolve around people.

Identifying Core Values

One of the best ways to go about identifying an organization's core values is to undertake a three-step process as an executive team. The first step is to identify the employees in the organization who already embody what is best about the company and to dissect them, answering what is true about those people that makes them so admired by the leadership team. Those qualities form the initial pool of potential core values.

Next, leaders must identify employees who, though talented, were or are no longer a good fit for the organization. These are people who, in spite of their technical abilities, drive others around them crazy and would add value to the organization by being absent. Once those people are identified—sadly, this is usually a little easier than the first step—they need to be dissected in the same way. What is it about them that makes them a distraction and a problem? It is the *opposite* of those annoying traits that provide yet another set of potential candidates for core values.

Finally, leaders need to be honest about themselves and whether or not they embody the values in that pool.

Mirror, Mirror

The leadership team of a fast-growing high-tech start-up asked me to help them identify their core values. After dissecting a handful of wonderful employees in the organization and then doing the same for some of the more difficult ones, the team was left with a few values that seemed like natural candidates for the core.

One of those values was friendliness. As simple as that may sound, the executives were convinced that it was what the best employees in the organization shared and what the difficult ones lacked. They decided that they would figure out a better way to describe friendliness in a way that would be more meaningful, but essentially, that was the concept they settled on.

It was then that I had to ask them to take the third step and ensure that their suggested core values, including friendliness, applied to them too. When I put the question to them, "So, would you say that this leadership team embodies friendliness?" the executives in the room hesitated a little and looked at one another. Without thinking too hard about it, I continued, "Because compared to the other teams I work with, I wouldn't say that you guys seem particularly friendly."

After a short pause, the executives laughed and agreed that they didn't really see themselves as overly friendly people either. And they quickly eliminated that from the list of core values. To call it part of their core would be to invite accusations of hypocrisy from employees. Imagine those executives standing up and touting the inherent friendliness of the company and building everything from performance reviews to hiring profiles around a concept that they did not exhibit naturally.

At the same time, the executives agreed that they needed to work on becoming more approachable and friendly, because it was something that many others in the organization valued. It would become an aspirational, but certainly not a core, value.

This three-step process is obviously not scientific, but it is nevertheless a reliable way of informing the judgment of leaders as they wrestle with what is core to the organization's culture. Settling on core values rarely happens in one sitting, and for good reason. It usually requires extended discussion and review among leaders who must be confident that their cultural building blocks are solid.

Having answered the first two questions, *Why do we exist?* and *How do we behave?,* a leadership team can then come down the mountain, so to speak, and begin answering the next four, which are a bit more concrete and tangible.

QUESTION 3: WHAT DO WE DO?

This question is the simplest of the six and takes the least amount of time and energy to address. The answer lies at the opposite end of the idealism scale from why an organization exists and is nothing more than a description of what an organization actually does. No flowery adjectives or adverbs here. Nothing ethereal or abstract. Just an unsexy, one-sentence definition—something your grandmother can understand (no offense to grandmas). The answer to this question is something we call an organization's business definition (but never a mission statement!).

If an organization's reason for existence answers the question, *Why?*, then its business definition answers the question, *What?* It's critical that it be clear and straightforward. It should not be crafted so that it can also be used in marketing material. The point is just to make sure that the leadership team is crystal clear about, and can accurately describe, the nature of the organization's business so that they don't create confusion within the rest of the company or, for that matter, in the market. It's as simple as that.

Coming up with a good business definition is usually not terribly difficult and often doesn't take much more than ten, maybe twenty minutes. Unlike the core purpose, most leaders have a good idea of the basic activities of the organizations they lead. Nevertheless, I'm always surprised when I ask members of a leadership team to quietly write down a sentence or two about what they think the organization does, and I find that there is more discrepancy than I or, more important, they had thought. Taking a few minutes to make sure everyone is on the same page is always worthwhile.

Here are a few examples from organizations we've worked with. They are not particularly interesting, and I suppose that's part of the point. They are simply concrete, detailed descriptions that, when combined with the reason for existing, describe what an organization does and why it does it:

105

- *A power company:* "We generate and deliver electrical and natural gas products and services to people throughout the state."
- *A credit card company:* "We provide payment products and extend credit to consumers."
- *A technology hardware company:* "We develop, manufacture, and market hard drives, solid-state drives, and storage subsystems for consumers, OEMs, and enterprises."
- *A biopharmaceutical company:* "We discover, develop, make, and commercialize better medicines through integrated sciences."
- *A Catholic church:* "We provide Sacraments, outreach services, counseling, and religious education for people in our parish."

Again, no adverbs or qualifiers, and no unnecessarily detailed descriptions of sales channels or pricing. That kind of information comes in the next section, when we get into strategy.

It should be noted that an organization's business definition can change over time, but only when the market changes and calls for a meaningful shift in the fundamental activity of the organization. In the course of my consulting firm's fifteen years as a company, we've changed our business definition three times. Keep in mind that our core values and reason for existing have never changed.

That's all that needs to be said about answering question 3, so that's all I'll say. The next question that needs to be answered is much more interesting and important.

QUESTION 4: HOW WILL WE SUCCEED?

When team leaders answer this question, essentially they are determining their strategy. Unfortunately, more than any word in the business lexicon, *strategy* is one of the most widely employed and poorly defined. Executives, consultants, and scholars use it to mean so many different things that it has become almost meaningless without a clarifying definition each time it is cited.

Years ago, not long after I started my consulting firm, a client asked me to help his team with its strategy, and I froze. I thought to myself, *What exactly is a strategy?* This was particularly troubling because I had spent two years working for a strategic management consulting firm. I wondered, *Did I sleep through the day they taught us the definition of strategy?*

So I went and did some research, reading and rereading a few books about strategy. And they were mostly confusing. Michael Porter's book, *Competitive Strategy*, was by far the most helpful, and using that and some of our own ideas based on companies we had worked with, we came up with our own definition and process for identifying strategy.[3] We were relieved, and a little surprised, to learn that clients found it to be so helpful, and that we weren't the only ones who were confused by the "s" word.

> An organization's strategy is nothing more than the collection of intentional decisions a company makes to give itself the best chance to thrive and differentiate from competitors.

Strategic Anchors

Essentially we decided that an organization's strategy is simply its plan for success. It's nothing more than the collection of intentional decisions a company makes to give itself the best chance to thrive and differentiate from competitors. That means every single decision, if it is made intentionally and consistently, will be part of the overall strategy.

But that definition is not particularly actionable or useful for guiding the decisions of leaders and employees. We came to realize that the best way for an organization to make strategy practical is to boil it down to three strategic anchors that will be used to inform every decision the organization makes and provide the filter or lens through which decisions must be evaluated to ensure consistency. Strategic anchors provide the context for all decision making and help companies avoid the temptation to make purely pragmatic and opportunistic decisions that so often end up diminishing a company's plan for success.

Strategic Branding

We worked with a fresh produce company that decided that one of its three strategic anchors was about maintaining "a premium, high-quality brand." As a result, the leaders marketed their products aggressively using the company name and they went to great lengths in stores to merchandise and present their higher-quality products in an attractive way to justify the higher prices that they commanded.

But sometimes the company's produce didn't come off the farm as attractive and delicious as they wanted it to be. Resisting the temptation to mix it in with the higher-quality product and hope that consumers wouldn't notice, the leaders decided to sell their slightly lower-quality produce through different channels and under a different brand and, of course, at a different price. And in those rare instances when they couldn't grow any premium-quality produce in a given category, the company simply refused to provide stores with products. Its leaders would rather forfeit short-term revenue than diminish the brand that they believed was critical to their differentiation and long-term success.

Keep in mind that another company with a different set of strategic anchors—namely, without a premium brand being one of them—would probably handle that situation differently. And that would be okay as long as it was intentional and consistent with what they believed would enable their success.

Identifying Anchors

The best way for leaders to go about finding their strategic anchors is to take a reverse-engineering approach and extract them from everything that they know to be true about their organization. They need to start by creating an exhaustive list of all the decisions and realities that form the context of their current situation. This will include anything beyond the organization's reason for existence, core values, and business definition.

To understand how this works, let's dissect a (mostly) fictional small, regional chain of sporting goods stores.

We'll assume that the company has already answered the questions, *Why do we exist?*, *How do we behave?*, and *What do we do?* Let's say their reason for existing is "to enable people to enjoy being outdoors," their core values are "enthusiasm for helping people, personal responsibility, and pride of ownership," and their business definition is, "We provide recreational and sports-related goods and equipment to people in the greater metropolitan area."

Having identified those critical components, the next question the leaders would need to answer, and the one at the heart of the strategic anchor activity, is, *How will we succeed?* Or put another way, *How will we make decisions in a purposeful, intentional, and unique way that allow us to maximize our success and differentiate us from our competitors?*

To create their exhaustive list, the leaders would consider everything imaginable related to their business. And I mean everything —topics like pricing, hiring, site selection, marketing, advertising,

109

branding, merchandising, sourcing, partnering, product selection, in-store experience, service offerings, promotions, decor, and more. I'm sure I've left a few things off that list.

Here's what their list looks like:

- Huge selection of products
- Competitive/low prices
- Nontraditional sports categories
- Seasonal focus of merchandise
- Informal, homemade signage in the stores
- Minimalistic displays and no glossy merchandising
- Free CPR and other medical classes
- Free meeting space for scouts and local sports teams
- Pet-related products
- Warehouse-like locations
- Easy access and parking
- Employee training and development opportunities
- Hire for attitude and cultural fit
- Seasonal employees
- Ski-lift tickets at cost
- Employee discounts
- Store stays open late
- Minimal advertising
- Active local event sponsorship
- Liberal return policy
- Flexible employment policies and hours
- Slightly better than industry-competitive wages and benefits
- Six stores in the metropolitan area
- High cooperation among stores
- Equipment rentals

That's a long and exhaustive list, and it needs to be. It's impossible not to notice that some of the items are slightly redundant and that there is no clear or consistent taxonomy. In other words, it includes apples, oranges, monkeys, and Cadillacs, which is fine. It's better to be redundant and a little inconsistent than to leave something out. The purpose is just to get everything out on the table (actually the flip chart) so that leadership team members can gain a sense of the whole messy picture. And it's worth noting that when we work with clients we don't write these items as a linear list. We draw a big amoeba-like shape on a flip chart and just start filling it in with terms and phrases. This makes it easier to see relationships between terms, which becomes important in the next step.

That next step is a little chaotic, difficult, unscientific, and fun. Leaders must search for patterns that would indicate the organization's strategic direction and anchors. Put another way, they need to identify the items, or collections of items, that fit together to form a theme or category. Michael Porter has a similar process called *activity system maps*.[4]

In the case of the sporting goods chain, there seems to be something common about having stores in large, low-rent buildings; spending minimal money on merchandising and signage; engaging in minimal advertising and traditional marketing; and charging relatively low prices. A leadership team might label this potential anchor, "keep prices low by being frugal whenever we can" or "reduce fixed costs as much as possible." Whatever they call it, it will speak to the idea of low prices and low costs.

Similarly, they would certainly see a connection between offering free CPR classes, free meeting space for local sports teams and scouts, easy access and ample parking, and sponsorship of local sporting events as something like "build local loyalty and become a community destination."

Finally, the competitive wages and benefits, investment in training, hiring for behavioral values, flexible hours and policies, employee discounts, and even the liberal return policy would suggest that "create a positive, flexible environment for employees" might be another anchor. (See "The Strategy Amoeba".)

Remember, this process will always be a little messy and organic. It requires judgment, reflection, and, at times, intuitive synthesis on the part of the members of a leadership team. Nonetheless, it is a reliable process that should lead to an outcome that will resonate with the team and inspire confidence in how decisions can be made in an intentional, strategic way.

The Strategy Amoeba

Keep prices low by being
frugal whenever we can

Create a positive, flexible
environment for employees

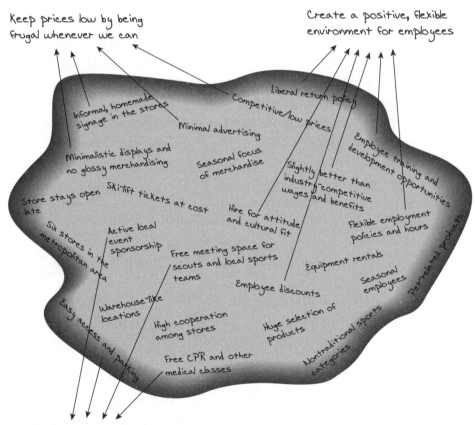

Liberal return policy

Competitive/low prices

Informal, homemade
signage in the stores

Minimal advertising

Minimalistic displays and
no glossy merchandising

Seasonal focus
of merchandise

Employee training and
development opportunities

Store stays open
late

Ski-lift tickets at cost

Slightly better than
industry-competitive
wages and benefits

Six stores in the
metropolitan area

Active local
event
sponsorship

Hire for attitude
and cultural fit

Flexible employment
policies and hours

Free meeting space for
scouts and local sports
teams

Equipment rentals

Seasonal
employees

Easy access and parking

Warehouse-like
locations

High cooperation
among stores

Employee discounts

Huge selection of
products

Pet-related products

Free CPR and other
medical classes

Nontraditional sports
categories

Build local loyalty and become
a community destination

Every organization's process for identifying strategic anchors will be different, though similarly messy.

Strategic Food

I was working with the confections division of a large food company. We started our strategy discussion by putting together an exhaustive list of truths about their business: integrated direct-to-store shipping model, a strong brand, customer-centricity, innovation, product quality (taste), leverage being part of a big company, operations as competitive advantage, compete against private label, part of parent company, superpremium brand, fun place to work, low margins, headquarters in New York, seven U.S. factories, high quality, U.S. market focus, complexity of operations, superior products, use of in-store marketing, multiple brands, consumer driven, and aggressive use of technology.

Next, the executives looked over the flip chart with all the items on it and searched for the potential anchors. To help them, we asked, "Which of these are so fundamental that they should be used as filters to inform every other decision?" The answers didn't leap off the page immediately, but, as usual, within five or ten minutes a few strong candidates began to emerge, as well as a few that were obviously not going to be strategic anchors (for example, headquarters in New York).

As people started to discuss the possible candidates for anchors, they came up with new and better ways to describe what they had originally put on the list, which was fine. We reminded them that this was a messy, nonlinear process, and that's the way it needs to be.

Whenever anyone made a recommendation for a possible anchor, we asked the team if that was fundamental, or if it was merely a function of something else on the list that

113

was even more fundamental. In the end, the team came up with the following strategic anchors: product superiority, in-store market execution, and predictable financial performance.

The team was saying that their success would be dependent on (1) continuing to make better-tasting and higher-quality products than their competitors, (2) being great at in-store merchandising and placement, and (3) delivering consistent and conservative financial results to their parent company. Every decision they made would need to be evaluated in light of and informed by these anchors.

For example, if a company emerged as a potential acquisition candidate, the team would evaluate that decision against the three criteria: (1) Does the acquisition candidate have products that are or could be of superior quality to those of their competition? (2) Can we merchandise those products in stores in a way that meets our high standards? (3) Is there a reasonable chance of seeing a profit in the not-too-distant future? If the answer to these questions is yes, it's probably a strategic fit. If the answers are no, going forward with the acquisition would probably not be a strategically aligned decision, regardless of how tempting it might be.

Now, in rare instances every organization will find itself in situations where it will have to make small, tactical short-term decisions that don't conform to its strategic anchors. It is critical that leaders be completely up front about the fact that such a decision is off-strategy and is a rare exception.

Unlike a company's reason for existing and core values, which never change, and the business definition, which changes fairly infrequently, an organization's strategic anchors should change whenever its competitive landscape shifts and market conditions call for a different approach.

How often this happens will vary depending on the nature of a given organization's market or industry (see the "Strategic Durability" sidebar below).

STRATEGIC DURABILITY

How often will your organization need to change its strategic anchors?

Well, that will depend largely on two industry traits: the barriers to entry in a given market and the rate of innovation.

When barriers to entry are high and innovation is relatively low, strategic anchors will be very durable and require less change over time. Airlines certainly fall into this category.

When barriers to entry are low and innovation is high, strategic anchors will need to be reviewed and revised much more frequently. Online software applications companies would fit this one.

When barriers to entry are high and innovation is high—something that would apply to pharmaceutical companies—strategic durability would fall somewhere in between. The same would be true when barriers to entry and innovation are both low, as is seen in many smaller services firms, including law, consulting, and advertising.

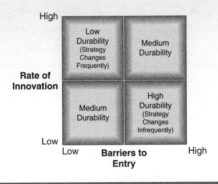

In some cases, one of an organization's strategic anchors may not yet be on the list because it isn't part of what the organization is currently doing, so it needs to be added. That's why it's important for an organization to realize that the process of identifying strategic anchors should not be completely reactive or historical. Sometimes it is the very process of identifying strategic anchors that alerts an organization to the fact that what it is currently doing isn't right or isn't enough to ensure success and differentiation, and so a change is needed.

Another outcome of establishing strategic anchors is making it easier to agree on what an organization should *not* be doing.

Strategic Schools

We worked with an organization that runs charter schools. As is true in many mission-driven organizations, there is a real temptation in schools for leaders to want to be all things to all people. Of course, with limited resources and high stakes, the cost of not being strategic is great.

The team started by creating an exhaustive list of everything that was currently true about the organization: focus on kindergarten through fifth grade, standardize core processes across all schools, headquarters in Texas, slightly lower staff pay than average public schools, emphasis on student safety, no transportation services provided, performance driven, data driven, no special education programs, emphasis on parent volunteerism and involvement, internal promotion of leaders, formative assessments, focus on benefit to kids, low cost, minimal branding and marketing, character-focused education, state-controlled pricing, distributed leadership model, local principal autonomy, no frills, employees passionate about mission.

After an hour of brainstorming and passionate debate, they arrived at the following strategic anchors: standardization of operations, selective marketing, performance and measurement driven. They decided that the way to ensure their success and differentiate from their competition was to ensure that every decision they made reflected (1) the ability to leverage standardized processes for efficiency and low cost, (2) to do only cost-effective, targeted marketing to parents in the micromarkets they served, and (3) to focus relentlessly on student achievement and parents' return on investment.

Those anchors also gave them the clarity about what they shouldn't do like provide transportation services and special education. As unhappy as they initially felt about those decisions, the leaders of the company knew that their ability to succeed in a competitive world meant they had to make difficult, strategic trade-offs.

Many leadership teams struggle with not wanting to walk away from opportunities that seem basically good and easily justifiable outside the context of having a strategy, but which would distract the organization and pull it away from its stated intent. Strategic anchors give a leadership team the clarity and courage to overcome these distractions and stay on course.

> Many leadership teams struggle with not wanting to walk away from opportunities. Strategic anchors give them the clarity and courage to overcome these distractions and stay on course.

Some people ask why there are three strategic anchors and not four or two or fifteen. Years ago I would have said, "Well, if you think having four or five works better for your organization, then go for it." But I've come to learn over the years, with the encouragement of clients and consultants who found it to be true, that there should be three anchors. I suppose there is something about the idea of triangulation that is at play here or the concept of the three legs of a stool. Maybe three is just the number of things that people can remember or keep in mind at any given time. Whatever the case, I'm convinced that three is almost always the right number of filters that an organization should establish to make their decision making as intentional as possible.

QUESTION 5: WHAT IS MOST IMPORTANT, RIGHT NOW?

More than any of the other questions, answering this one will have the most immediate and tangible impact on an organization, probably because it addresses two of the most maddening day-to-day challenges companies face: organizational A.D.D. and silos.

Most organizations I've worked with have too many top priorities to achieve the level of focus they need to succeed. Wanting to cover all their bases, they establish a long list of disparate objectives and spread their scarce time, energy, and resources across them all. The result is almost always a lot of initiatives being done in a mediocre way and a failure to accomplish what matters most. This phenomenon is best captured in that wonderful adage, "If everything is important, nothing is."

When a CEO announces that her company's top priorities for the year are to grow revenue, improve customer service, introduce more innovative products, cut expenses, and improve market share (we've all seen lists like this before), she is almost guaranteeing that none of those objectives is going to get the attention it deserves. And there is an additional consequence beyond the distraction, diffusion, and dilution that this causes: the emergence of departmental silos.

By communicating that the organization has five or seven top priorities, leaders put their well-intentioned employees in the inevitable position of getting pulled in different directions, sometimes polar opposite ones. Wanting only to succeed, they often find themselves working at cross-purposes with their colleagues in other departments who are left to make their own decisions about which of the many priorities is most important. Leaders should not be surprised to find that the various departments within the organization are operating as independent units without alignment and cooperation.

One Thing

Of course, to say that there are too many top priorities is something of an oxymoron. After all, for something to be the *top* priority, it has to be more important than everything else. And even if there are multiple big priorities, ultimately one of those has to be at the very top. The point here is that every organization, if it wants to create a sense of alignment and focus, must have a single top priority within a given period of time.

> Every organization, if it wants to create a sense of alignment and focus, must have a single top priority within a given period of time.

I came to realize this somewhat by accident. I had been hearing so many of my clients complain about the silos within their organizations that I decided I should try to solve that problem. So I went out in search of companies where silos were not an issue to learn from them. It was a dry search.

Then I realized that there was a certain category of organization that seemed to rise above the silo problem: emergency responders. These include firefighters on the scene of a fire, emergency room doctors and nurses, soldiers on a rescue mission, and even police officers in the midst of a dangerous situation. Silos just didn't seem to exist in these groups.

Think about it. You never see two firefighters standing in front of a burning building and arguing about which one of them should be responsible for climbing up and saving a child's life based on the departmental jurisdiction of their respective divisions. And you aren't going to find two nurses debating which cost center to bill for gauze while a patient in the ER is hemorrhaging blood. And in the midst of a battle, you aren't going to hear a Marine say, "I'm not going to risk my life. This is a Navy problem."

Of course, what these groups have in common is a crisis—a clear and present situation of great and immediate consequence. What a crisis provides for an organization, whether that organization is an emergency responder accustomed to dealing with crises or a more traditional organization that finds itself temporarily in the midst of one, is a rallying cry, a single area of focus around which there is no confusion or disagreement.

The Thematic Goal (a.k.a. The Rallying Cry)

As I thought about the power of a rallying cry, I wondered why all organizations couldn't replicate the benefits of achieving that kind of focus (short of creating false crises, which is never a good idea). And I decided that there is no reason that every organization couldn't have a rallying cry, even when it is not in crisis. I called this rallying cry "a thematic goal" because it needs to be understood within the context of the organization's other goals, at the top of the list. And so, the thematic goal is the answer to our question, *What is most important, right now?*

I introduced this concept in one of my business fables, *Silos, Politics, and Turf Wars*, which may be helpful for readers wanting to see a thorough and vivid description of the thematic goal concept.[5] Before I provide a few real world examples, I'll clearly define what a thematic goal is so that all of this makes sense:

A thematic goal is . . .

- **Singular.** One thing has to be *most* important, even if there are other worthy goals under consideration.
- **Qualitative.** The thematic goal should almost never be established with specific numbers attached to it. The opportunity for putting quantitative measures around a thematic goal comes later, and it should not be done too early because it can too narrowly prescribe what needs to be achieved and limit people's ability to rally around it.
- **Temporary.** A thematic goal must be achievable within a clear time boundary, almost always between three and twelve months. Anything shorter than three months feels like a fire drill, and

anything longer than twelve invites procrastination and skepticism about whether the goal will endure. *(I'll wait a few months to focus on that because it will probably change, and, who knows, I might not even be working here then.)*

- **Shared across the leadership team.** When executives agree on their top priority, they must take collective responsibility for achieving it, even if it seems that the nature of the goal falls within one or two of the executives' regular areas of ownership.

The best way to identify a thematic goal is to answer the question, *If we accomplish only one thing during the next x months, what would it be?* In other words, *What must be true x months from now for us to be able to look back and say with any credibility that we had a good period?* These questions provide a critical level of focus for leaders who are being pulled in numerous directions.

Once a team has agreed on its thematic goal, it should resist the temptation to run out and communicate that goal right away or make a big announcement about it. For one, the thematic goal alone is not enough. It needs further detail or it will come across as an empty campaign slogan. I'll get to that shortly.

Second, the primary purpose of the thematic goal is not necessarily to rally all the troops within the organization, as helpful as that may seem. More than anything else, it is to provide the leadership team itself with clarity around how to spend its time, energy, and resources. Yes, in most cases, it will be appropriate for leaders to eventually communicate that goal to employees at large or to some subgroup of them. In rare cases, when the thematic goal revolves around a confidential matter like a potential merger or layoff, it will not. That will depend on the nature of the goal and the extent to which it involves a concerted, wide-reaching effort throughout the company. But even if the leadership team never announces the thematic goal to anyone and uses it only to guide its own actions, it will have served its purpose.

Leaders Without Hats

Regardless of how it is communicated within the larger organization, it's worth repeating that every thematic goal must become the collective responsibility of the leadership team. This is true even if the goal doesn't seem to directly involve the departments that some of those executives lead. To understand what this means, it's helpful to think about members of the executive team going into each of their meetings without their departmental titles. Or as I like to say, they need to take off their departmental hats and put on generic corporate ones. I explored this basic idea in my description of team number one in the "Build a Cohesive Leadership Team" section, but it's certainly worth repeating here.

On a cohesive team, leaders are not there simply to represent the departments that they lead and manage but rather to solve problems that stand in the way of achieving success for the whole organization. That means they'll readily offer up their departments' resources when it serves the greater good of the team, and they'll take an active interest in the thematic goal regardless of how closely related it is to their functional area. And while individual team members will certainly have expertise and responsibility in different parts of the business, they will not limit their input and participation to those areas alone. Unfortunately, on many teams, this happens regularly.

Like the representatives of Congress or the United Nations, too many leaders come to meetings with the unspoken assumption that they are there to lobby for and defend their constituents. When they see that the agenda for a staff meeting has little if anything pertaining to their world, they do their best to avoid conversation in the hope that the meeting will end quickly. Or they try to sneak in some busywork to attend to or perhaps even shift the focus of the meeting to something that involves them and their department.

This is a perfect recipe for dysfunction and mediocrity. And while I'll address the subject of meetings later in this book, let me make it clear that it is the lack of a defined, compelling rallying cry or thematic goal that allows most bad staff meetings to happen, which enables poor decision making.

The benefits of establishing an overarching thematic goal are enormous. Divisional rivalry and infighting become much less likely as leaders stop seeing their primary responsibility as solely running their own departments. Focus during meetings gets easier as unimportant and ancillary topics are guiltlessly cast aside. Paralysis around resource allocation can be broken due to clarity around what deserves the most energy and attention. And the need to referee political battles, not only at the executive level but deeper in the organization, diminishes greatly as people better understand the trade-offs that need to be made and the rationale for them.

Defining Objectives

Realizing the benefits of having a clear and collective focus requires more than merely identifying the thematic goal. That goal must then be further clarified by defining the objectives which will make accomplishing it possible. I call these, for obvious reasons, defining objectives. (I originally wanted to call them "big buckets of stuff" but was overruled by my wiser colleagues.)

Defining objectives are the general categories of activity required to achieve the thematic goal. Like the thematic goal, defining objectives must be qualitative, temporary, and shared by the leadership team. They provide a level of specificity so that the thematic goal isn't merely a slogan but rather a specific and understandable call to action. In most cases, there are between four and six defining objectives, depending on the nature of the goal itself.

Mail Priorities

We were working with the leadership team of a large freight and logistics company that was doing very well. However, among the various challenges that the leaders were discussing was a problem with having no excess capacity to take on the growing volume of business that was coming their way. After discussing this and various other topics competing for their attention, we posed the big question: *If you accomplish just one thing in the next nine months, what should it be?*

Within just a few minutes, the team agreed that "if we don't solve the capacity issue, we're in huge trouble."

So "solve the capacity problem" became their thematic goal. Not sexy, but clear and correct. And just as important, there was no ambiguity that this thematic goal would become the top priority of every team member, regardless of their specific functional responsibilities.

The next step was to define exactly what they would need to do to address the problem and achieve the thematic goal. After less than an hour of discussion and debate, they came up with the following defining objectives:

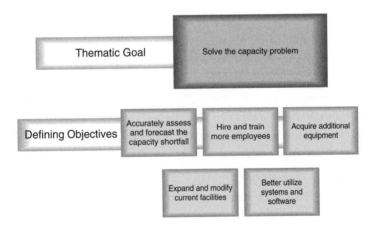

(We use the graphic above to depict thematic goals and defining objectives because it is easier for leaders to remember and display for future reference.)

As obvious as this may seem in retrospect, had the executive team not had this conversation, they would have gone back to work and continued working on whatever projects and responsibilities they usually attended to, treating the capacity problem as just another of a long list of important objectives. Instead, they ended the conversation ready to talk about what they should stop working on, and how they would reallocate less-critical resources in the organization to accomplish the thematic goal.

But the team wasn't done.

Standard Operating Objectives

Once teams identify their defining objectives, they have to take on the next, and last, step in the thematic goal process: identifying their standard operating objectives. These are the ongoing and relatively straightforward metrics and areas of responsibility that any leadership team must maintain in order to keep the organization afloat. I like to refer to these responsibilities as the "leaders' day jobs."

Coming up with standard operating objectives is not terribly difficult because they are usually somewhat obvious. In for-profit companies, they usually include categories like revenue, expenses, customer retention or satisfaction, product quality, cash flow, morale, or any other issues specific to a given industry. In a hotel, it would certainly include room occupancy, in a school it would include graduation rates and test scores, and in a church it might well include attendance and financial giving. Whatever the case, few leadership teams need more than fifteen minutes to identify and agree on their standard operating objectives, which are already a big part of their daily focus.

In the previous example, the freight company's standard operating objectives would include revenue, expenses, on-time deliveries, customer satisfaction, new customer acquisition, safety, and morale.

My small consulting firm tracks the following standard operating objectives: financial strength (revenue and expenses are included), staff morale, book sales, product sales, consulting pipeline, speaking pipeline, client satisfaction, and stewardship. Every company will have a slightly different set of standard objectives that it tracks, but it will be relatively predictable and consistent depending on the industry and it won't change much over time.

It's important to note that sometimes a company's thematic goal will be one of the items that appears on its standard operating list. For instance, a hotel will regularly track occupancy, but in a given period that issue may become its most critical challenge. So the leaders would elevate it to the top of their list and make "increase occupancy" their thematic goal for a period of time. And if the freight company we worked with found that accidents and workers' compensation claims were affecting its financial viability, the leaders might well make "improve safety" their thematic goal for a period of time, even though it is always on their standard operating objectives list.

That's not to say that most thematic goals come from the standard list, just that it is sometimes what is called for. And, of course, once the thematic goal has been achieved, the item goes back on the standard list.

The One-Page Model

Different kinds of organizations have different thematic goals, defining objectives, and standard operating objectives for a variety of reasons. However, what they all have in common is that their goals fit on a single sheet of paper.

Credit Card Focus

One of our consultants worked with an affiliate credit card company that was constantly developing partnerships with

127

organizations to co-brand their credit cards with them. They brought on a large and strategically critical new partner, an airline that was going to try to migrate as many of its frequent flyer mileage credit cards over to our client.

The executives felt themselves being pulled in various directions and pressured to constantly bring in new business, even while they lamented the possibility of failing to adequately service the new airline partner. Finally, they agreed on a thematic goal that would provide them with the focus and alignment they needed:

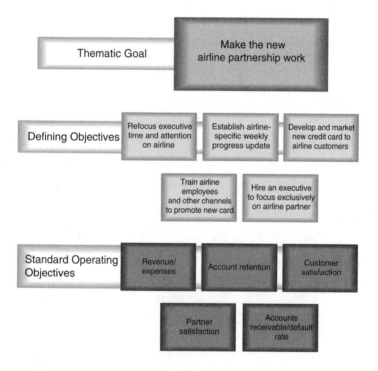

Walking away with a single sheet of paper that lists a team's thematic goal, the defining objectives, and the standard objectives would give leaders the clear focus they need to align their actions and avoid distraction.

Shedding a Reputation

We worked with the leadership team of an IT organization in a huge health care company. For years, IT had been viewed poorly within the organization, despite the efforts of the CIO and her team to avoid mistakes and defend the department when things didn't go well. The department had been criticized for failing to deliver projects on time, not providing levels of service adequate for the lines of business, and being generally unresponsive to the needs of the company.

When the team learned about the thematic goal concept, they decided that it was time to rally around the goal of finally shedding their reputation for underperformance. Their thematic goal image looked like this:

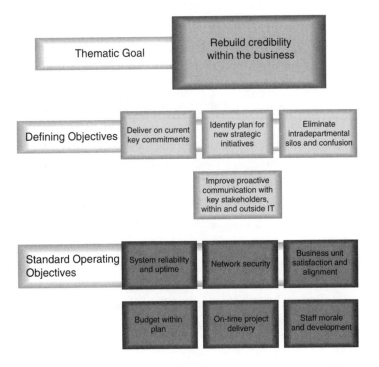

Within a year of establishing this thematic goal framework, the team turned around its reputation internally, as measured by customer surveys and stakeholder feedback from executives. What is more, for the subsequent eight years, the department has been able to maintain its new reputation as successful and reliable. The CIO explained, "It wasn't until we made this our explicit top priority and got clear about exactly what we had to do that we were able to rally together and turn things around."

The length of time that a thematic goal should live (within the 3–12 month time frame) is up to the leadership team and depends on the reality of how much time a given issue requires addressing. Having said that, the size of the organization and the nature of its business will have a big impact on the time period during which a thematic goal endures. Small companies and start-ups usually find that shorter time periods are more appropriate because they can get more done in less time and they have less cushion and permission to make mistakes. On the other side of the equation, large organizations, especially schools and government entities, usually have longer planning cycles and tend toward lengthier thematic goals.

As the time frame for accomplishing a thematic goal grows near, a leadership team will want to start thinking about the next one. Of course, a measure of flexibility is important. If a team makes faster progress than expected toward a thematic goal, then they should come up with their next one sooner. And if, after a few weeks or months, they decide that the thematic goal is no longer appropriate or that something else has become more important, they should certainly shift to a new one.

Remember, the purpose of having a thematic goal is not to restrict the organization's flexibility but rather to rally its leaders around what they decide they want to achieve.

Once a leadership team has identified its thematic goal, defining objectives, and standard operating objectives, it has one last question to answer, and it's probably the easiest of them all.

QUESTION 6: WHO MUST DO WHAT?

Although I just made it clear that executives must come to meetings without their departmental hats on and that they must be prepared to engage in achieving the thematic goal of the team regardless of their areas of expertise, at some point the leaders need to clearly and unambiguously stipulate what their respective responsibilities are when they go back to work to do their day jobs. The fact is, every organization of any size needs some division of labor, and that begins at the very top. Without clarity around that division of labor, the potential for politics and infighting, even among well-intentioned people, is great.

There is not a great deal to be said about this particular question, aside from warning leadership teams not to take it for granted. Although there is often clarity among executives in most organizations about who does what on the team, making assumptions about that clarity can lead to surprising and unnecessary problems.

Part of the challenge is that most organizations have adopted conventional titles for their various departments. Depending on the industry, most have some combination of many of the following roles: head of sales, marketing, finance, operations, human resources, engineering, IT, customer service, and legal. And while those functional descriptions are pretty good indicators of the general responsibilities of members of the leadership team, I'm always a little surprised when I ask them all to quietly write down their descriptions in some level of detail.

Often members of the team will be surprised at what they learn from their colleagues during this short exercise. Sometimes two people claim to be responsible for the same task or discipline: "Hey, I have business development on my list too!" In other cases, there will be a gap: "How come no one has strategic planning on their list?"

In many cases, it's the leader of the executive team, often the CEO, who presents the biggest problem. Many of these leaders take on active roles beyond their responsibility of managing the leadership team, and this can create confusion. For instance, in many smaller organizations, the founder and CEO occupies two separate roles: leader of the executive team and functional specialist.

The Two-Headed CEO

One of the first organizations I consulted to was a start-up fashion apparel company that operated out of a small warehouse with five employees. The CEO was the original product designer. As the company experienced rapid growth and market acceptance, he promoted one of his earliest employees to be head of products (the guy was actually the company's original shipping administrator and janitor who turned out to be a remarkable designer).

The problem, of course, was that the CEO continued to function as the chief product specialist, which had the potential for creating confusion for everyone on the team, not the least of which was the new head of products. During meetings, when the CEO weighed in on product issues, team members didn't push back much because they mistakenly assumed he was speaking as the CEO and declaring his intention to make a final decision. In reality, he was just weighing in as a product designer and hoping to encourage discussion.

Realizing that he was inadvertently squelching debate and overriding the authority of his head of product development, the CEO decided he had to be more explicit with his team during meetings about which role he was playing and whether his intention was to contribute to the conversation or drive closure as the organization's chief executive.

133

It's tempting for leaders, especially those at the top of organizations, to temporarily step into roles where they are talented or comfortable. What they often don't realize, however, is that others in the organization, even on their team, aren't as clear as they are about where lines of responsibility ultimately lie.

Regardless of how clear or confusing a company's "org" chart may be, it is always worthwhile to take a little time to clarify so that everyone on the leadership team knows and agrees on what everyone else does and that all critical areas are covered.

Okay, let's assume a team has successfully answered each of the six critical questions. They can still fail to benefit from the clarity they've achieved if they don't capture that clarity effectively.

THE PLAYBOOK

Once the leadership team has answered each of the six critical questions, it is absolutely critical for them to capture those answers in a concise, actionable way so that they can use them for communication, decision making, and planning going forward.

Leaders usually make one of two mistakes after leaving an off-site meeting or a strategy session where they've agreed on something important. Often they capture their decisions in a glossy, bound document and then place it on a shelf to gather dust. Or they do nothing to capture their ideas, assuming that the people in the room will naturally glean the ideas that are important or relevant for their departments.

The best alternative to these extremes and the most effective tool for keeping key decisions alive is the creation of something we refer to as a playbook: a simple document summarizing the answers to the six critical questions. While every organization will, and should, create a playbook that is customized to their needs, there are two things that the leaders of any organization should do to make their playbook work.

First, they must keep it short. Anything more than a few pages is unnecessary and discourages people from reviewing the playbook. In most cases, the answers to the six questions can be captured on a single page—two at the most. And even if a team wants to add information from Discipline 1 (build a cohesive leadership team), like team member profiles and results from the team effectiveness exercise, no more than three pages will be needed.

Second, leadership team members should keep their playbook with them at all times. And not buried in a briefcase. They should keep it on their desks, bring it to staff meetings, and have it available for quick reference and as a tool for communicating to employees.

The following is an example of a company playbook. But remember that whatever form it takes, the key is to keep the answers to the six critical questions alive and accessible. By doing this, a leadership team will drastically improve the odds of running the organization in an aligned, consistent, and intentional way.

Playbook Example

Lighthouse Consulting

Why do we exist? We exist because we believe the world needs more great leaders.

How do we behave? We behave with passion, humility, and emotional intelligence.

What do we do? We provide services and resources for leaders who want to make their organizations more effective.

How will we succeed? We will differentiate ourselves by providing extremely high-touch service, staying relatively small and protecting our unique culture, and leveraging the ideas of world-class subject matter experts.

What is most important, right now?

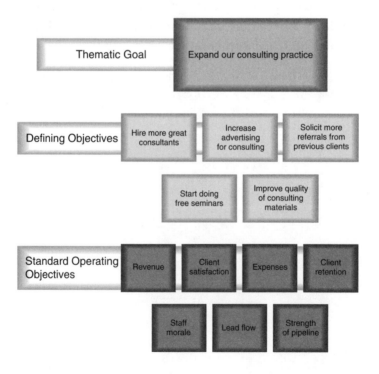

Who must do what?

Name	Title	General Responsibilities
Michael	CEO	Executive team leadership, company strategy, key sales support
Dick	Consulting Ops	Consultant and project management, content development
Amy	CFO	Finances, IT, legal, general administration
Matt	Sales	Standard sales, partnerships
Tom	Marketing	Standard marketing, customer education, events
Christa	HR	Training, benefits, compensation

Team profile

Name	Type	Areas for Improvement
Michael	ENTJ	Interrupt less; follow through on commitments
Dick	INTP	Engage more with peers; respond more quickly to inquiries/e-mails
Amy	ISTJ	Explain things more thoroughly; speak up during meetings
Matt	ENFP	Stay focused and on-topic during meetings; follow through
Tom	INFJ	Don't be afraid to disagree; be tougher on your staff
Christa	ESTJ	Flex more to business needs; don't be defensive about department

CHECKLIST FOR DISCIPLINE 2:
CREATE CLARITY

Members of a leadership team can be confident that they've mastered this discipline when they can affirm the following statements:

— Members of the leadership team know, agree on, and are passionate about the reason that the organization exists.

— The leadership team has clarified and embraced a small, specific set of behavioral values.

— Leaders are clear and aligned around a strategy that helps them define success and differentiate from competitors.

— The leadership team has a clear, current goal around which they rally. They feel a collective sense of ownership for that goal.

— Members of the leadership team understand one another's roles and responsibilities. They are comfortable asking questions about one another's work.

— The elements of the organization's clarity are concisely summarized and regularly referenced and reviewed by the leadership team.

WHAT'S IT WORTH TO YOU?

Back to those two organizations.

The first is run by a leadership team whose members regularly remind employees about the company's reason for existence, its core values, its strategy, and its top priority. They leave meetings clear about what they've agreed to do and what they're going to go back and tell their employees. They also take steps to ensure that they know the concerns and ideas of the people in their organizations so that they can represent and consider them when making decisions.

The second has a leadership team that limits its communication to a few events each year, and even then the focus is mainly on tactical goals and initiatives. Their messaging after meetings is often sparse and inconsistent, and they aren't particularly aware of the opinions of the employees deeper in their organizations.

The question: What kind of advantage would the first organization have over the second, and how much time and energy would it be worth investing to make this advantage a reality?

Overcommunicate Clarity

O nce a leadership team has become cohesive
and worked to establish clarity and alignment around the answers to the six critical questions, then, and only then, can they effectively move
on to the next step: communicating those answers.
Or better yet, overcommunicating those answers—
over and over and over and over and over and over
and over again.

That's right. Seven times. I've heard claims that
employees won't believe what leaders are communicating to them until they've heard it seven times.
Whether the real number is five, seven, or seventy-
seven, the point is that people are skeptical about
what they're being told unless they hear it consistently over time.

That need for repetition is not a testament to
undue cynicism on the part of employees; it is the

result of the generic, almost spoof-like communication that takes place within so many organizations. Scott Adams and his Dilbert character have built a cottage industry around highlighting the clichés at the heart of this phenomenon, and I wish I could say that the comic strip was way off base.

After all, just about every leader says that *quality is job number one, the customer is king,* and *employees are the organization's greatest asset.* It's almost comical how rote these messages have become. And so it's not surprising that employees give little credence to executive pronouncements and instead wait to see how serious those executives are. One of the best tests of seriousness is whether they continue to repeat themselves over a prolonged period of time.

Unfortunately, most leaders I've worked with are hesitant to repeat themselves. They call to mind that old wives' tale (it really is a wives' tale), where a woman asks her husband, "Why don't you tell me you love me anymore?" The husband seems a little surprised by the question and after considering it for a moment replies, "Well, I told you I loved you when we got married. I'll let you know if it changes."

Leaders inadvertently do the same thing when they walk away from an annual all-hands meeting and think that they've done their job of communicating by giving a speech outlining the organization's strategy or priorities. And they think they've been especially thorough when they announce that the slides for the presentation can be found on the company's intranet site. But then they seem surprised when they learn, a few weeks later, that employees aren't acting on what they were told and that most of those employees can't even repeat the organization's new strategy accurately.

The problem is that leaders confuse the mere transfer of information to an audience with the audience's ability to understand, internalize, and embrace the message that is being communicated. The only way for people to embrace a message is to hear it over a period of time, in a variety of different situations, and preferably from different people. That's why great leaders see themselves as Chief Reminding Officers as much as anything else. Their top two priorities are to set the direction of the organization and then to ensure that people are reminded of it on a regular basis. So why do so many leaders fail to do this?

Many don't enjoy the reminding role because it seems wasteful and inefficient to them. They've been trained to avoid redundancy in virtually every aspect of their work, so embracing it in communication isn't easy for them. But some leaders aren't so much worried about the wastefulness of overcommunication; they fear that repeating a message might be insulting to their audience. They assume that employees don't need to be told something more than once and that they'll feel patronized if they are.

> Great leaders see themselves as Chief Reminding Officers as much as anything else.

What those leaders fail to realize is that employees understand the need for repetition. They know that messaging is not so much an intellectual process as an emotional one. Employees are not analyzing what leaders are saying based solely on whether it is intellectually novel or compelling, but more than anything else on whether they believe the leaders are serious, authentic, and committed to what they are saying. Again, that means repetition is a must.

Finally, many leaders fail to overcommunicate because they get bored saying the same things over and over again. This is understandable. Intelligent people want to be challenged with new messages and new problems to solve, and they get tired of revisiting the same topics. But that doesn't matter. The point of leadership is not to keep the leader entertained, but to mobilize people around what is most important. When that calls for repetition and reinforcement, which it almost always does, a good leader relishes that responsibility.

Repetition is more than just a matter of communicating something again and again in the same way. Effective communication requires that key messages come from different sources and through various channels, using a variety of tools. This includes assorted electronic media, from e-mail to videoconferencing to whatever funky new communication technology is being introduced to the market when this book goes to print. However, the most effective means of communicating a message, even in a large and far-flung organization, has nothing to do with technology and has been around since the beginning of time. What I'm referring to is word of mouth.

CASCADING COMMUNICATION

Someone once told me that the best way to ensure that a message gets communicated throughout an organization is to spread rumors about it. Therefore, they concluded, leaders simply ought to go out and tell "true rumors." As silly as that may sound, it is the basis for the most important means of communication within a healthy organization.

> If the best way to ensure that a message gets communicated throughout an organization is to spread rumors about it, then leaders simply ought to go out and tell "true rumors."

The most reliable and effective way to get an organization moving in the same direction is for members of a leadership team to come out of their meetings with a clear message about what was decided, promptly communicate that message to their direct reports, and have those direct reports do the same for their own direct reports. We call this "cascading communication" because it begins the structured but interpersonal process of rolling key messages down through the organization directly from the leadership team.

If this sounds ridiculously simple, that's because it is. And yet it doesn't happen in the vast majority of companies in spite of the fact

144

that it is so effective. Part of the reason for its effectiveness has to do with its contrast to more formal means of communication. Over the past fifteen or twenty years, employees have grown accustomed to inconsistent, untimely, and manufactured electronic communication from their leaders. That's not meant to sound cynical; it's just a reality. Most leadership teams are more than adept at sending out e-mail messages and giving presentations, and yet they still struggle with effective communication because employees wonder about the authenticity of what they are reading and hearing.

Cascading communication provides a great opportunity to change all that. Amazingly, when employees in different parts of an organization hear their leaders saying the same things after meetings, they actually start to believe that alignment and clarity might be possible. This allows a leadership team to get a quick and meaningful win, one that creates momentum for executives and employees alike.

Consistent Messaging

One of my earliest clients was a global software company that had offices in just about every part of the world. Unsurprisingly, employees in different offices felt disconnected from one another, regardless of how many e-mail announcements, videoconference messages, and company T-shirts they received.

And then the executive team started doing cascading communication, leaving their meetings and going back to their direct reports with a common set of messages. Those direct reports were then charged with relaying those same messages to their teams.

I remember the day that the woman who headed HR in Australia called her colleague in Germany to tell him about something her boss had just told her that was happening at corporate. Shocked, her German colleague said, "Hey, my boss just told me the same thing!" They felt a greater sense of alignment because of that one simple instance of consistent, informal messaging than they did after receiving any of the other more produced forms of communication.

There are three keys to cascading communication: message consistency from one leader to another, timeliness of delivery, and live, real-time communication. This starts toward the end of leadership team meetings, a time when executives are usually trying their best to get out the door. That's when someone needs to ask the sixty-four-thousand-dollar question: "Hey, what are we going to go back and tell our people?"

For the next few minutes, sometimes longer, leaders need to review their discussions from the meeting and decide which of their decisions are ready to be communicated and which are not. We refer to this as "commitment clarification," for obvious reasons. Often it's during this process that they discover that they were not on the same page about what they thought they had decided. Only then can they get real clarity by settling on the decisions they've made and agreeing to go out and spread true rumors about them. This will certainly take more time, but the cost of not doing it is often great.

Postmeeting Confusion

I worked for a company early in my career that was struggling and needed to cut costs. After a long executive staff meeting, it was decided that there would be a freeze in hiring new employees until the revenue situation at the company had been improved.

The head of human resources left the staff meeting and sent out a worldwide e-mail message announcing the hiring freeze. Within five minutes, two of her peers who had been in the meeting were in her office protesting the new policy.

"I didn't think the freeze applied to sales!" pleaded one executive. The other executive chimed in. "And there's no way that we're going to cut back on engineers, are we?"

The team was put in the position of having to retract its announcement and amend its policy, which created tension among team members, not to mention a loss of credibility in the eyes of employees. All of this because they didn't take a few minutes to get clear about what they were really committing to at the end of a staff meeting.

As important as alignment is, what teams shouldn't do is word-smith those messages to death and make themselves sound like robotic leaders going out to read from the same exact script. Instead, they need to get clear on the main points to communicate and then go to their teams to explain those points in their own words.

It's critical that leaders do this during a short and consistent time frame. If one member of the team goes back to her staff to convey the messages right after the meeting and someone else waits a week to do so, there will be understandable confusion and disappointment among employees. That's not to say that it has to happen in the same moment. However, a twenty-four-hour period following a meeting is not a bad standard.

Many executives ask if they can communicate the results of a meeting using e-mail or even voice mail. The answer is no. Although these tools are certainly more efficient than having to communicate live, they are drastically less effective. For one, employees don't have a chance to ask questions for clarification. Moreover, when employees read an e-mail or listen to a voice mail, they can't help but wonder how the message was edited, and they try to read between the lines to discern the underlying meaning.

The best way to do cascading communication is face-to-face and live. Seeing a leader and hearing the tone of his or her voice is critical for employees, as is being able to ask a question or two. Having said

147

that, the realities of virtual teams and geographically dispersed employees sometimes make face-to-face communication impossible. That's when a telephone call or a videoconference is a good idea. The key is that the discussion is live and interactive.

Another good idea when doing cascading communication, whenever it's possible, is to do it with an entire group of direct reports at the same time instead of one by one. Aside from being more efficient, it ensures that they hear the same message at the same time and benefit from one another's questions and observations.

As I write this, I'm all too aware that the advice I'm giving might sound extremely basic. But then again, most organizations are unhealthy precisely because they aren't doing the basic things, which require discipline, persistence, and follow-through more than sophistication or intelligence.

Beyond the simple discipline of doing cascading communication after every leadership team meeting, leaders can ensure that key messages are effectively disseminated throughout an organization in a few other ways. The first and most important is to incorporate the answers to the six critical questions in any situation that calls for leaders to be communicating with employees—everything from recruiting, interviewing, orienting, managing, rewarding, training, to even dismissing people from the organization. We'll cover many of these in the next chapter on reinforcing clarity.

But before doing that, let's review a simple framework for understanding the various ways in which communication flows in a healthy organization.

TOP-DOWN COMMUNICATION

This is the most common direction that critical information travels in an organization, and the various tools used to do it include all-hands meetings, employee newsletters, regular e-mail announcements, social media, and, of course, cascading communication. I won't go into detail about these here, because there are plenty of books and articles, not to mention consulting firms, that have more information and knowledge than I do about these various forms of basic communication.

What I will say is that the reason most organizations fail to communicate to employees is not that they don't know how to build an intranet site or write a blog or design a Power-Point presentation, but that they don't achieve clarity around key messages and stick with them. The world is full of organizations where employees feel uninformed and in the dark even though they have access to more glossy newsletters, interactive Web sites, and overly produced employee meetings than they need or want. What they don't get is consistent, authentic, and relevant communication.

> The world is full of organizations where employees feel uninformed and in the dark even though they have access to more glossy newsletters, interactive Web sites, and overly produced employee meetings than they need or want.

Keeping It Real

One of the best exemplars of effective top-down communication that I've seen was the CEO of a large health care company who sent out a one- to three-page e-mail message to all employees every Friday. What was particularly amazing was not the volume of his communication but the authenticity, directness, and relevance of his messages.

As the organization went into a difficult period, the CEO used those Friday e-mail messages to keep employees focused and motivated around the difficult job ahead of them. Any employee at the company, regardless of their department or level, had access to the unedited and often vulnerable insights of their leader. The company was able to weather the storms they faced, and the overcommunication of their CEO was a big reason for this success.

Of course, it's worth repeating that the success of top-down communication starts with Discipline 1 (build a cohesive leadership team) and Discipline 2 (create clarity). Without these, no amount of communication is going to be effective.

UPWARD AND LATERAL COMMUNICATION

Providing employees with a means of communicating upward to their leaders is important in any organization. However, it's not the panacea it's often presented to be. That's because noncohesive leadership teams that have not aligned themselves around common answers to critical questions are not in a position to respond adequately to employee input and requests. In fact, getting more input from employees often only exacerbates frustration in an organization when that input cannot be digested and used.

Still, there is something to be said for providing people in an organization with channels for upward communication, whether that takes the form of employee surveys or roundtable discussion forums. What is key to making these effective is that leaders not give the impression that they are abdicating responsibility for decision making by giving employees a vote. Great organizations, unlike countries, are never run like a democracy.

It's also critical for leaders to realize that no upward communication program will ever take the place of a manager who understands and represents the views of his or her employees. It shouldn't be used to overcome the shortcomings of leaders who are out of touch with their people.

One of the most common complaints in unhealthy organizations has to do with breakdowns in communication across departments or divisions. And as much as leaders might want to implement special communication programs to alleviate this, the only good way to address it is to attack the root cause: unresolved issues among the leaders of those divisions. The most well-intentioned, well-designed departmental communication program will not tear down silos unless the people who created those silos want them torn down.

Finally, it's worth noting here that some of the healthiest organizations I've known don't do a lot of formal upward or lateral communication, and some of the least healthy ones are mired in employee surveys, executive listening forums, and departmental conferences. This is a testament to the fact that without cohesiveness and clarity at the top, no amount of communication will suffice, and that with true clarity and cohesiveness, even a little formal communication will go a long, long way.

CHECKLIST FOR DISCIPLINE 3: OVERCOMMUNICATE CLARITY

Members of a leadership team can be confident that they've mastered this discipline when they can affirm the following statements:

- The leadership team has clearly communicated the six aspects of clarity to all employees.
- Team members regularly remind the people in their departments about those aspects of clarity.
- The team leaves meetings with clear and specific agreements about what to communicate to their employees, and they cascade those messages quickly after meetings.
- Employees are able to accurately articulate the organization's reason for existence, values, strategic anchors, and goals.

WHAT'S IT WORTH TO YOU?

Those two organizations one final time.

The first has simple, practical processes for recruiting, hiring, and orienting the right people based on its core values, for managing those people's performance around the organization's most important priorities, and for rewarding and training them based on the company's culture, strategy, and operations. Moreover, managers embrace those processes and find them to be helpful tools for succeeding in their jobs.

The second has plenty of processes and human systems, but most of those are generic and cumbersome and not customized to the unique culture and operations of the company. As a result, managers find them largely frustrating and irrelevant to their work.

The question: What kind of advantage would the first organization have over the second, and how much time and energy would it be worth investing to make this advantage a reality?

Reinforce Clarity

As important as overcommunication is, leaders of a healthy organization cannot always be around to remind employees about the company's reason for existing, its values, and so on. In order to ensure that the answers to the six critical questions become embedded in the fabric of the organization, leaders must do everything they can to reinforce them structurally as well. The way to do that is to make sure that every human system—every process that involves people—from hiring and people management to training and compensation, is designed to reinforce the answers to those questions.

The challenge is to do this without adding too much structure. Or as someone once said to me, "An organization has to institutionalize its culture without bureaucratizing it." There is a delicate but critical balance between too much and too little structure in an organization, and the people responsible for creating that balance are its leaders.

> An organization has to institutionalize its culture without bureaucratizing it.

Unfortunately, all too often leaders don't take an active role in designing human systems. Instead, they delegate responsibility to others in the organization, usually to their HR department or legal staff. It amazes me that they later complain about the bureaucracy in their organizations, like having to do onerous and tedious performance reviews.

Blaming HR and legal for all this is neither fair nor helpful. The problem can be solved only by the leadership team taking an active role in building human systems that reflect and reinforce the uniqueness of the organization's culture and operations. They must ensure that hiring profiles, performance management processes, training programs, and compensation systems are relevant, and the only way to do that is to design them specifically around the answers to the six questions.

NON-GENERICS

Many well-intentioned executives will argue that HR professionals have more expertise and experience in building human systems than members of the leadership team do, and therefore they should take responsibility for it. While that is true, those HR folks can't be expected to fill the role that their leaders must perform in these areas.

Don't get me wrong. HR and legal professionals play important roles in the creation and administration of human systems. But the initial design of those systems must be driven by the people who set the direction for the organization in the first place and have the authority to guard against the bureaucracy that turns a useful human system into an administrative distraction. When leadership team members abdicate responsibility for this, they are often left with more generic, rote systems and processes than they wanted.

Some leaders actually embrace this in the name of efficiency and standardization, believing that if a performance review system or compensation plan "is good enough for General Electric or PepsiCo, then it's good enough for us." The problem is, they aren't leading GE or Pepsi. (Anyone working for GE or Pepsi can ignore this.)

The fact is that the best human systems are often the simplest and least sophisticated ones. Their primary purpose is not to avoid lawsuits or emulate what other companies are doing but rather to keep managers and employees focused on what the organization believes is important. That's why a one-page, customized performance review form that managers embrace and take seriously is always better than a seven-page, sophisticated one designed by an organizational psychologist from the National Institute for Human Transformation and Bureaucracy (there is no such thing).

This point cannot be overstated. Human systems are tools for reinforcement of clarity. They give an organization a structure for tying its operations, culture, and management together, even when leaders aren't around to remind people. And because each company is different, there are no generic systems that can be downloaded from the Internet.

> Human systems give an organization a structure for tying its operations, culture, and management together, even when leaders aren't around to remind people.

Let's take a quick look at the most important human systems that an organization needs, according to the logical life cycle of an employee.

RECRUITING AND HIRING

Bringing the right people into an organization, and keeping the wrong ones out, is as important as any activity that a leadership team must oversee. Though few leaders will dispute this, not many organizations are good at doing it, for a variety of reasons.

First and foremost, too many organizations have not defined exactly what the right and wrong people look like; that is, they haven't clarified a meaningful set of behavioral values that they can use to screen potential employees. I addressed this when I discussed core values, but it's worth repeating. Hiring without clear and strict criteria for cultural fit greatly hampers the potential for success of any organization. And even for organizations that have identified the right set of behavioral values, a host of other problems keep many of them from hiring well.

For all the talk about hiring for fit, there is still too much emphasis on technical skills and experience when it comes to interviewing and selection. And this happens at all levels. When push comes to shove, most executives get enamored with what candidates know and have done in their careers and allow those things to overshadow more important behavioral issues. They don't seem to buy into the notion that you can teach skill but not attitude.

And even organizations that have defined their core values and really do believe that those values should trump everything else sometimes lose their way when it comes to ensuring cultural fit because they don't have the right kind of process for hiring. I've found that most companies fall into one of two categories on opposite sides of the structural scale for hiring.

Gut Feel Versus Structure

Many leaders, especially those who run smaller organizations, believe that they have the natural skills they need to choose good people without any real process. They look back at their careers and remember the good employees they've hired and give themselves credit for having recognized those people's potential. However, they seem to block out the memories of the unsuccessful hires they've made, or they justify those mistakes based on the hidden behavioral deficiencies in the people they later had to fire. Whatever the case, they persist in the belief that they know a good person when they see one and that they can go about the hiring process without much structure.

The screening, interviewing, and evaluation process that exists in these leaders' organizations tends to be not much of a process at all. Although résumés may be closely scrutinized before bringing a candidate in for interviews, the interviews themselves are often unstructured and unplanned. There is little preparation, if any, and no real strategy for identifying the critical signs that indicate a candidate will be successful.

It's truly stupefying to think that the most important decision a leader can make—who to invite to become a part of the organization—is often handled in such a cavalier way. One of the reasons this persists, I think, has to do with the considerable time lag between when a bad hiring decision is made and when everyone realizes the problem. Somehow leaders fail to make a cause-and-effect connection between their initial lack of a rigorous interviewing process and the spotty record of quality hiring that comes about as a result. I've become convinced of this because I've seen too many leaders who, even after admitting that they made a bad hire, fail to change their approach.

The other extreme, though slightly less common, doesn't yield much better results. When organizations overstructure their hiring process by adding layers of bureaucratic forms and approvals and analysis, they often diminish the role that judgment must play in the selection of good people. This is more common in larger organizations, where an overemphasis on administrative processes seems to hinder the ability or desire of hiring managers to use common sense and discernment. Often it is a well-intentioned human resource or legal department that drives these efforts.

Like all subject matter experts, HR departments often try to employ the most sophisticated, state-of-the-art processes, which often leads them to adopt an overly complicated or academic approach to hiring. This might make sense theoretically, but it is usually difficult to teach managers to adhere to such a process on a large scale. Legal departments, for their part, are usually and understandably focused on avoiding lawsuits that can arise as a result of the interview process or even afterward in the event that an employee is terminated. So they do their best to eliminate subjectivity, which often means judgment, by adding more and more structure. In both cases, the insistence on too much process overshadows the real goal of any effective hiring program: finding people who fit the culture and have the best chance at success.

The best approach to hiring is to put just enough structure in place to ensure a measure of consistency and adherence to core values—and no more. That's right. When it comes to the continuum of hiring, ironically, I find that it is better to be somewhere closer to having a little less structure than more. I believe this because too much structure almost always interferes with a person's ability to use their common sense, and because it is far easier to add a little structure later to a fairly bare system than it is to deconstruct an already overcomplicated process.

What might this more balanced approach look like? First, it should probably take no more than one page, front and back, to describe and apply. One side explains the process, along with a description of the core values and related behaviors that indicate a person is a good fit for the organization. This provides interviewers and hiring managers with a list of the observable and discernible traits that must be confirmed or denied in the interview and selection process. The other side of the page can be used for taking notes about the candidate during the interview.

Second, all of this should be consistent across departments within an organization. Sure, engineers and marketers and salespeople are going to have different technical requirements for employees in their areas, which may require them to have another page or two for their unique criteria. But when it comes to overall cultural fit—by far the most important hiring priority for the leaders of any organization—using a single, simple, consistent process across departments is critical.

Interviewing

Once the values and the forms and any other simple collateral have been created, a process must be put in place for using them. And again, that process must have some structure for the sake of consistency, but more important, it must be simple and flexible.

When it comes to the actual practice of interviewing, many leaders still make the same mistakes that they did forty years ago. First, they have the candidate sit across a desk from them while they ask questions about their résumé. Second, they don't do enough joint planning with other interviewers and end up asking many of the same questions that everyone else is going to ask. Third, they don't debrief thoroughly with the other interviewers but instead just send a vague and cursory "thumbs up" or "thumbs down" to whoever is organizing the process.

Because the purpose of an interview should be to best simulate a situation that will give evaluators the most accurate view of how a candidate really behaves, it seems to me that getting them out of the office and doing something slightly more natural and unconventional would be a better idea. Heck, even taking a walk or going shopping is better than sitting behind a desk. The key is to do something that provides evaluators with a real sense of whether the person is going to thrive in the culture of the organization and whether other people are going to enjoy working with him or her.

Hiring for Fit

One large company that is legendary in its hiring practices, as evidenced by its bottom-line performance and the long line of candidates who want to work there, took a unique approach to weeding out people who wouldn't fit the culture. That culture was built around a healthy sense of self-deprecation and humility.

In the process of interviewing a group of people for a job that requires great responsibility and technical ability, the candidates (all of whom happened to be men) were asked to exchange their formal suit pants for a pair of khaki shorts. This meant they would be spending the rest of the day walking around the corporation's headquarters wearing suit jackets, ties, dress shoes, dark socks, and shorts! They looked silly, to say the least.

A handful of those candidates found the situation beneath them and insulting. Some were visibly uncomfortable, and a few others decided to leave and opt out of the process. The company's reaction to all this was relief; they had successfully identified those people who, though technically qualified, did not fit the culture. While some might consider this process to be humorously cruel, it is actually a great service to the job candidates and the organization. It prevented a number of people from having to endure a painful and unsuccessful employment experience, and it prevented the happy employees who already worked at the organization from seeing the culture they love diluted. And that's to say nothing of the money it saved the organization by avoiding unnecessary turnover.

Of course, the only way to make all this work is for evaluators to get together after interviewing candidates to hash out what they observed and what collective conclusions they've come to.

160

There are plenty of books that delve into specifics about hiring and interviewing, so I don't need to go into any more detail here. However, I will repeat, yet again, that without a clear understanding of what a cultural fit—or misfit—looks like, without a proper mix of consistency and flexibility, and without the active involvement of the leadership team, even the most sophisticated hiring process will fail.

> Without a clear understanding of what a cultural fit or misfit looks like, and without the active involvement of the leadership team, even the most sophisticated hiring process will fail.

ORIENTATION

The most memorable time of an employee's career, and the time with the biggest impact, are his or her first days and weeks on a new job. The impact of first impressions is just that powerful, and healthy companies take advantage of that to move new employees in the right direction. That means orientation shouldn't revolve around lengthy explanations of benefits and administration but rather around reinforcing the answers to the six critical questions.

When employees get the opportunity to hear their leaders talk about why the organization they joined exists, what behavioral values were used to select them during the hiring process, how the organization plans to succeed, what its top priority is, and who does what at the executive level, they can immediately see how they will contribute to the greater good of that organization. This often sets the tone for their behavior and attitude during their entire tenure with the company and sends them home from work boasting about the professionalism and promise of the company they're now a part of.

Contrast this with the way so many organizations handle orientation. Rather than seeing it as the first opportunity to reinforce the most important messages of the firm, they delegate responsibility to administrative functions that will naturally focus on, well, administrative functions. And while that may help the new employee understand how to fill out insurance paperwork and use the new e-mail system (both of which are surely helpful), it tends to be a disappointment to anyone who joins an organization because they're excited about having the opportunity to make a real difference in some way.

Leaders of organizations, even very large organizations, need to understand the value of bringing in new employees with clarity, enthusiasm, and a sense of their importance. It is an opportunity that disappears within days or weeks of a new employee's arrival and should never be wasted.

There are many ways to handle orientation, and I don't need to go into them here because there is no one right way to do it. What is key is that it is built around the six questions and that leaders take an active role in its design and delivery. That's probably enough about orientation.

PERFORMANCE MANAGEMENT

Nothing has the potential for bureaucracy and wonkiness like performance management systems. Even the term itself is fuzzy and generic enough to send a busy manager into a process coma. And so I suppose it needs to be defined.

Essentially *performance management* is the series of activities that ensures that managers provide employees with clarity about what is expected of them, as well as regular feedback about whether or not they are adequately meeting those expectations. That may be a bit simple, but that's the heart of the idea, and it really ought to be simple. Unfortunately, few organizations are good at performance management, mostly because they are confused and inconsistent about why they do it in the first place.

Over the years, as the litigiousness of society has grown, leaders have become more fearful that employees who are fired will sue the company and bleed them of scarce financial resources. This is understandable when we consider the exorbitant cost, in time and money, of having to mount a legal defense, even if we eventually win. So legal departments have tried to use the performance management process to protect the company legally. They've insisted that managers master the art of detailed documentation and record keeping, something that can be used to derail a lawsuit before it gets too expensive.

As logical as this might seem, the unintended consequences have been devastating. Most important, employees and managers alike have come to see the performance management process as a largely adversarial activity, fraught with nervous negotiation rather than clear communication. Ironically, this has probably exacerbated the legal problems of organizations more than mitigated them. When employees focus more on the official "grades" they receive from managers, and managers focus on documentation more than coaching, inevitably trust is diminished and management and communication suffer.

Healthy organizations believe that performance management is almost exclusively about eliminating confusion. They realize that most of their employees want to succeed, and that the best way to allow them to do that is to give them clear direction, regular information about how they're doing, and access to the coaching they need. Healthy organizations also realize that even the most rigorous systems cannot prevent all lawsuits and that sacrificing the real purpose of their performance management system to prevent them, even if that were possible, is a bad trade-off.

The best performance management programs—you guessed it—are simple. Above all else, they are designed to stimulate the right kinds of conversations around the right topics. Those topics are some of the same ones I have addressed in achieving organizational clarity: goals, values, and roles and responsibilities. When organizations build simple, straightforward performance management programs, they make it much easier for managers to use them more frequently. This is a good thing because it provides regular reminders for employees about what is important and builds greater trust by preventing too much time from passing between meaningful conversations.

> The best performance management programs are designed to stimulate the right kinds of conversations around the right topics. That's all.

Another part of the overall performance management system has to do with corrective action and documentation of warnings before an employee can be terminated. This is messy and nasty and, unfortunately, necessary. I'll leave this topic for the lawyers and HR folks who understand it best. However, I will say that it is critical that organizations separate corrective action processes from the regular performance management system, because the last thing an organization wants is for its good employees to feel as if they're being interrogated and prepared for dismissal.

COMPENSATION AND REWARDS

Don't worry. I'm not going to go into much detail about this subject. Again, there are many books on the topic and consultants who know much, much more about the technical aspects of compensation and rewards systems than I do. The point that needs to be made here is that the single most important reason to reward people is to provide them with an incentive for doing what is best for the organization.

Yes, this sounds patently obvious, but somehow most companies' compensation and rewards programs get divorced from this purpose, and take on a disconnected life of their own. When that happens, they lose their value and actually become sources of distraction rather than tools of focus and motivation.

Members of a leadership team must take responsibility for ensuring that compensation and rewards programs are simple, understandable, and, most important of all, clearly designed to remind employees what is most important. This is especially true at the executive level because the way that leaders themselves are rewarded and compensated will inevitably have an impact on how they motivate their people.

At the core of any of these systems must lie the answers to the six critical questions. For instance, when employees are given a raise, they need to understand that they are being rewarded for behaving or performing in a way that is consistent with the organization's reason for existing, core values, strategic anchors, or thematic goal. And when employees are denied a raise or a bonus, they need to understand that it is because they did not behave or perform in a way that is consistent with all those things. These are great moments of truth for leaders to demonstrate that they are really committed to what they say is important. To fail to make the connection between compensation and rewards and one or more of the six big questions is to waste one of the best opportunities for motivation and management.

I realize that not every compensation decision is easy to connect to a specific performance or behavior that ties to one of the six big questions. And I realize that sometimes an employee gets a two percent raise because that's all that his or her manager could get for that person. In those situations, it is critical that leaders are clear with employees about the disconnect between performance and financial reward and that they work to eliminate that disconnect.

165

RECOGNITION

As important as compensation and rewards are, they aren't the most effective or important means of motivating people in a healthy organization.

Real-Time Recognition

One of our consultants was working with the leadership team of a nonprofit company that was focused on finding ways to reinforce the company's values through rewards and recognition, both formal and informal. As the leaders were discussing the various employees in the organization, one woman, a very junior employee, was mentioned for her amazing work on a big project and how she had clearly demonstrated the company's values.

Our consultant asked the company's leadership team, "So, have you told this woman that she's doing a great job and that you think of her as an example of what you want from other employees?" Much to the consultant's surprise, the executives sheepishly shook their heads.

"Okay, let's bring her in here." The executives in the room wondered if he meant what he said, so he continued. "I'm serious. Go get her right now, and tell her the things that you just told me about her."

A few minutes later, the woman came into the room where the executive team was meeting. She seemed confused, and even a little petrified, about why her presence had been so urgently requested, especially when they asked her to take a seat in the front of the room facing the entire team.

For the next few minutes, the team asked her questions about what she had done and gave her a chance to explain the project and her role in it. Then they began telling her how much they appreciated her actions and how she had been a real role model for the rest of the organization in living the values.

Clearly emotional, the woman almost cried. After she collected herself, thanked the team, and left, our consultant didn't need to say much. He just asked the leaders if they thought that woman would continue to be a champion of the values. Of course, they agreed she would, and they committed to doing more direct, informal recognition in the future.

I like to explain to clients that when leaders fail to tell employees that they're doing a great job, they might as well be taking money out of their pockets and throwing it into a fire, because they are wasting opportunities to give people the recognition they crave more than anything else. Direct, personal feedback really is the simplest and most effective form of motivation.

So why isn't this more common? For one, many leaders convince themselves that employees are motivated primarily by money. As a result, they discount the impact of authentic and specific expressions of appreciation and focus instead on financial rewards like raises and bonuses. Additionally, I think many leaders are a little embarrassed by giving praise and are afraid that employees will discount it as a cheap replacement for financial rewards.

> Many leaders convince themselves that employees are motivated primarily by money. As a result, they discount the impact of authentic and specific expressions of appreciation.

What leaders need to understand is that the vast majority of employees, at all levels of an organization, see financial rewards as a satisfier, not a driver. That means they want to receive enough compensation to make them feel good about their job, but additional money doesn't yield proportionate increases in their job satisfaction. And while they're not going to turn down an offer of more money, that is not what they're really looking for. In fact, gratitude, recognition, increased responsibilities, and other forms of genuine appreciation are drivers. That means an employee can never really get enough of those and will always welcome more.

Most organizations simply assign too much importance to financial compensation and too little to the other side of the equation. They often do this because they believe that people who leave their organizations are doing so because they want more money. This is an understandable mistake because that is what many employees say during exit interviews when they've already made up their mind to leave. However, almost no employees willingly leave an organization where they are getting the levels of gratitude and appreciation that they deserve just to make a little more money, unless, of course, they are so grossly underpaid that they can't justify staying in the job for the sake of their livelihood.

Anything for Retention

A friend of mine worked for a management consulting firm for about six years. He was paid well, but after putting up with as much neglect and politics as he could stand, he finally decided to leave.

When he was called in for his exit interview with a senior manager who had never taken an interest in him before, he was asked, "What could we have done to keep you here longer?"

My friend was a little stunned by the hollowness of the question. After a moment, he just smiled and replied, "Anything."

I tell this story not only because it demonstrates the importance of nonfinancial factors in job satisfaction, but also because I think it's funny.

The lesson for leaders is not that they should be cheap, but rather that they understand that the healthiest organizations in the world are not necessarily the highest-paying ones and that throwing money at a problem that would be better solved through improved management is a true waste of resources. What is more, unsatisfied employees who receive greater financial compensation as an incentive to stay in an unhealthy organization feel cheapened by the gesture. And they are usually just as determined to eventually find a better place to work.

FIRING

When I think about firing as a human system, I'm not thinking about it so much in terms of the administrative process that an organization goes through to let someone go. That's not to say that this isn't important; the way people are treated as they leave an organization is critical because of how it affects their life and because of the message it sends to the rest of the organization about how its leaders view people.

But when it comes to building a healthy organization, the most important part of the firing process is the very decision to let someone go. That decision needs to be driven, more than anything else, by an organization's values.

In a healthy organization, a leader who is thinking about letting someone go will evaluate that person against the entirety of the company's values, paying special attention to the core and permission-to-play varieties. If an employee's behavior is consistent with the core and permission-to-play values, there is a good chance that it would be a mistake to let him go. Essentially he has the raw material to fit into

169

the organization and be successful. Instead of firing him, the company should take a closer look at how he is being managed and find a way to give him a chance to succeed.

But if the leaders of an organization are clearly convinced that an employee does not fit the core or permission-to-play values, even if he meets basic performance criteria, they would be advised to gracefully help that person find employment elsewhere.

Keeping a relatively strong performer who is not a cultural fit creates a variety of problems. Most important of all, it sends a loud and clear message to employees that the organization isn't all that serious about what it says it believes. Tolerating behavior that flies in the face of core values inspires cynicism and becomes almost impossible to reverse over time. When leaders take the difficult step of letting a strong performer go because of a values mismatch, they not only send a powerful message about their commitment to their values, they also usually find that the performance of the remaining employees improves because they are no longer being stifled by the behavior of their former colleague.

> Keeping a relatively strong performer who is not a cultural fit sends a loud and clear message to employees that the organization isn't all that serious about what it says it believes.

Addition by Subtraction

Years ago before I started my own consulting firm, I hired a talented guy to join my department. My staff and I were overwhelmed with projects, and I was relieved to have found someone who could lighten the load. He proved to be both competent and hard working, but it was apparent that he didn't share my department's values of teamwork and selflessness. Still, buried with work, I made one of the worst mistakes of my career: I promoted him!

Fortunately, my staff members weren't afraid to tell me that I had blatantly violated our values by rewarding someone who wasn't a cultural fit. I couldn't deny the boneheadedness of what I had done, and decided that I would have to manage the guy to become a better team player.

In just a few weeks, it became clear that he just wasn't interested and that his need for attention was a fundamental part of his personality. Still, he was a talented and productive worker. So I helped him find another job within the larger organization, in a department where his personality and values would be a fit.

Beyond restoring my credibility with my staff members, something very powerful happened: the performance of my team improved substantially. Without that one colleague, someone who clearly didn't fit the department's humble, selfless culture, the rest of the team's excitement and commitment soared. It was a profound lesson, one that I won't forget.

Finally, keeping someone who clearly doesn't fit culturally is almost always a disservice to that person, who knows that he doesn't belong and is usually as frustrated as his colleagues are. Letting him go is putting him in a position to find an organization where he does belong and where he'll be able to thrive.

CHECKLIST FOR DISCIPLINE 4:
REINFORCE CLARITY

Members of a leadership team can be confident that they've mastered this discipline when they can affirm the following statements:

— The organization has a simple way to ensure that new hires are carefully selected based on the company's values.

— New people are brought into the organization by thoroughly teaching them about the six elements of clarity.

— Managers throughout the organization have a simple, consistent, and nonbureaucratic system for setting goals and reviewing progress with employees. That system is customized around the elements of clarity.

— Employees who don't fit the values are managed out of the organization. Poor performers who do fit the values are given the coaching and assistance they need to succeed.

— Compensation and reward systems are built around the values and goals of the organization.

The Centrality of Great Meetings

An organization that has embraced each of the four disciplines will certainly become healthy, making success highly likely. But one activity, more than any other, will be central to maintaining those disciplines, and sustaining health, over time.

No action, activity, or process is more central to a healthy organization than the meeting. As dreaded as the "m" word is, as maligned as it has become, there is no better way to have a fundamental impact on an organization than by changing the way it does meetings.

In fact, if someone were to offer me one single piece of evidence to evaluate the health of an organization, I would not ask to see its financial statements, review its product line, or even talk to its employees or customers; I would want to observe the leadership team during a meeting. This is where values are established, discussed, and lived and where decisions around strategy and tactics are vetted, made, and reviewed. Bad meetings are the birthplace of unhealthy organizations, and good meetings are the origin of cohesion, clarity, and communication.

If someone were to offer me one single piece of evidence to evaluate the health of an organization, I would want to observe the leadership team during a meeting.

So why in the world do we hate meetings? Probably because they are usually awful. More often than not they are boring, unfocused, wasteful, and frustrating. Somehow we've come to accept this—to believe that there is just something inherently wrong with the whole idea of meetings. It's almost as though we see them as a form of corporate penance, something that is inevitable and must be endured.

Well, I am utterly convinced that there is nothing inherently bad about meetings, nothing that can't be fixed if we confront the problems we've allowed to grow and calcify over the years. I wrote about those problems in a fictional way in my book *Death by Meeting*.[1] In that book I addressed a concept at the heart of the problem with meetings, something I call "meeting stew."

MEETING STEW

A good way to understand meeting stew is to imagine a clueless cook taking all of the ingredients out of the pantry and the refrigerator and throwing them into one big pot, and then wondering why his concoction doesn't taste very good. Leaders do the same thing when they put all of their issues into one big discussion, usually called a "staff meeting." All too often they combine administrative issues and tactical decisions and creative brainstorming and strategic analysis and personnel discussions into one exhausting meeting. And like that cook, somehow they are surprised when the result doesn't turn out so well.

The fact is that the human brain isn't meant to process so many disparate topics in one sitting. There needs to be greater clarity and focus, which means that there needs to be different kinds of meetings for different kinds of issues. And, yes, that means there will be more meetings, not fewer.

That's right. Leaders who want healthy organizations cannot try to eliminate or reduce time spent in meetings by combining them or cutting them short. Instead, they have to make sure that they are having the right kinds of meetings, and then they must make those meetings effective. As a result—and trust me when I say this—leaders actually come to look forward to their meetings, even enjoy them. In fact, they get real work done during those meetings which makes their lives, and the lives of their employees, better as a result.

THE FOUR MEETINGS

So what kinds of meetings does the leadership team of a healthy organization have? There are four basic types:

Content		Timing
Administrative	Daily Check-In	5–10 minutes
Tactical	Weekly Staff	45–90 minutes
Strategic	Adhoc Topical	2–4 hours
Developmental	Quarterly Off-Site Review	1–2 days

1. Daily Check-Ins

The first category of meetings is the least important but certainly worth doing when it is practically possible. Essentially, it's about the team getting into the habit of gathering once a day, for no more than ten minutes, to clear the air about anything administrative that would be helpful to know. Schedules. Events. Issue alerts. That kind of stuff.

There are no agendas and no resolution of issues, just an exchange of information. To make sure that these meetings don't morph into something they shouldn't, it's even best if people don't sit down. The purpose of these daily administrative check-ins is simply to get the team accustomed to talking on a regular basis and to provide a forum for addressing the uber-tactical kinds of issues that get in the way of more important issues at staff meetings.

Plenty of leadership teams will protest having to do daily check-ins. Some of their reasons are valid, others not.

A good reason *not* to do daily check-ins is that members of the team are so spread out geographically that it isn't practical to expect them to get together every day. That's not to say that some virtual teams don't find a way to do this by phone. But when it takes heroic efforts on the part of people in multiple time zones to make a daily conference call work, it can become just another form of drudgery. In those cases, not doing them is fine.

When team members work in the same location, there are no good reasons for rejecting the daily check-in. But what if some team members are out of the office? Have the session without them and let them know they can call in if they're able. No pressure. What if people have other meetings during that time? First, don't schedule meetings during that ten-minute period, but in the odd event that it is inevitable, don't worry about it. Everyone else can meet. What if people feel they are too busy? That's a bad excuse. Here's why.

The most powerful impact of having teams meet every day is the quick resolution of minor issues that might otherwise fester and create unnecessary busywork for the team. For instance, when teams members don't see each other more than once a week, or even less often, they end up trying to resolve the endless administrative issues that surface every day with an e-mail here and a voice mail there and a hallway conversation in between. That sets off a flurry of more e-mails, voice mails, and hallway stops as the situation changes and more people on the team need or want to be looped in. It would be fascinating to actually track and calculate the amount of time and energy that leaders spend chasing down issues that could be sorted out in a thirty-second conversation if everyone were in the same room for a few minutes every day.

A big part of the beauty of the daily check-in is that leaders know they're going to see their colleagues within twenty-four hours, so rather than firing off an e-mail or a voice mail or interrupting someone in the course of their day, they simply make a note to bring up a small issue at the next day's meeting. There is something undeniably efficient and liberating about this, which makes the protests I hear from executives all that much more absurd. It's as though they're saying, *Do you realize how busy we are trying to solve problems that result from our lack of communication? We can't possibly spend ten minutes every day preventing them!*

Once teams get used to the daily check-in, they're hooked.

Disconnected

The leadership team at a Silicon Valley company implemented the daily check-in begrudgingly at first. Then, after a few weeks, they got used to the activity and did it gladly without complaint. Still, they didn't completely understand the value of it.

Then, during one particular period when a large number of leadership team members were on vacation, the daily check-ins came to a halt. As so often happens, when everyone came back to work, the discipline of the daily meeting didn't get reestablished.

After a few weeks, team members felt strangely disconnected, and after talking about it, they realized that the cause was not having the daily sessions. The president of the company explained what happened: "We never realized how much closer we were to each other, and how much we were able to avoid wasting time and energy, until we stopped having the daily check-ins."

Getting used to doing the daily meeting will probably take a few weeks or a month. But once it happens, leaders find that they're building stronger relationships with their peers much more quickly than they thought was possible. Moreover, they're able to address minor issues quickly so they can be more focused on the right topics during the other three kinds of meetings they need to have.

2. Tactical Staff Meetings

When executives complain about meetings, many of them are probably thinking about their weekly or biweekly or monthly staff meetings. This is where meeting stew is usually served.

The truth is, there is no more valuable activity in any organization than the regular staff meeting of a leadership team. But if they are not effective, there is little or no chance of building a cohesive team or a healthy organization.

There are a few critical keys to making staff meetings work, many of which I've already discussed in this book. For instance, if there are too many people on a team, or if the people in the room don't trust each other and aren't willing to engage in productive conflict, then no matter how you reorganize your meetings you won't see much impact.

However, assuming that a leadership team has bought into and is working on making their team small enough and behaviorally cohesive, they then need to change a few things about what they do before and during their staff meetings to make them compelling, useful, and yes, even enjoyable.

Real-Time Agenda

The first thing a team must do to improve their staff meetings is really about what they should stop doing before the meeting. I'm referring to the dreaded agenda. Putting together an agenda before a staff meeting is like a marriage counselor deciding what issues she's going to cover with a couple prior to meeting with them. The fact is, you don't know what you need to discuss until you've come together and assessed the situation.

Instead of putting together an agenda ahead of time, team members need to come together and spend their first ten minutes of a meeting creating a real-time agenda. That involves two steps.

First, the leader needs to go around the room and ask every member of the team to take thirty seconds to report on the two or three key activities that they believe are their top priorities for the week. Notice that I said "that they *believe* are their top priorities." See, it's possible that after everyone explains what they're doing and the team assesses what's going on in the organization, people are going to have to reorder their priorities.

Once everyone has taken their thirty seconds to list off, not expound on, their top priorities—most will use only ten or fifteen seconds—the leader moves on to the second part of creating a real-time agenda. This entails reviewing the one-page scorecard or chart that the team created—the one that includes their thematic goal, their defining objectives, and their standard operating objectives. I covered that simple structure in Discipline 2 when I discussed the question, *What is most important, right now?*

Tactical Meeting Scorecard

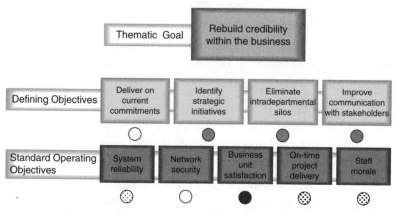

Green = open circle   Yellow = medium-shaded circle   Red = dark-filled circle
Lime green = light-dotted circle   Orange = heavy-dotted circle

Essentially this part of the meeting is about stepping back and asking, *How are we doing against the things we said are most important?* And the way teams evaluate themselves is by using an easy and digestible means of assessing progress: colors. That's right. No matter how much data an organization has at its disposal, no matter how intelligent and sophisticated the members of a team may be, the key to quickly sizing up the organization's progress and deciding where to spend scarce resources is by keeping the evaluation process as simple as possible. I don't know of a better system than green for "things are good, we're ahead of schedule," yellow for "we're doing okay, but we're not yet where we ought to be," and red for "we're way behind on this one." (Okay, we allow teams to use lime green and orange for those in-between evaluations.)

It should take a team only five or ten minutes to go through the items on their scorecard, assigning a color to each item. Different people will influence each decision based on their perspective, and that's good. In fact, leaders always learn a great deal about what is happening when they hear their colleagues' assessments. "I'd give us a green on

180

revamping our marketing message," says one executive. "Are you kidding?" says another. "Did you see the results of that focus group last week?" The first executive's eyes go wide. "No, I didn't. What did they say?" The second exec explains, "They threw up all over our ideas. We're back to square one." And everyone agrees that the color is red.

After the team has assigned their colors—a process that really is as enjoyable as it is informative—then and only then can they agree on what their agenda should be. Basically they will probably focus on the areas on the chart that are red or orange or perhaps one or two others that are particularly critical.

The beauty of this real-time agenda system is that the team will avoid the all-too-common problem of sitting through a presentation or a discussion of something that everyone knows is of little importance to the organization. When leaders put together agendas ahead of time, they're often influenced by people in the organization who do a good job lobbying them for face time at the next staff meeting. Before anyone knows what's happening, they're sitting in a forty-five-minute multi-media presentation about how the HR department selected a vendor for the benefits program, even when the company's benefits program is nowhere near being worthy of making it on the scorecard. Of course, if the company is experiencing employee turnover because of benefits and that is one of the critical issues facing the team, then by all means they should bring in the director of benefits. But leaders must make that decision because it warrants the time and energy of the leadership team, not because it seemed like a considerate thing to do for someone who wanted some extra attention.

A challenge that many leadership teams struggle with during staff meetings is the distraction that occurs when someone raises a compelling and important topic that shouldn't be taken on during tactical meetings. While this may seem like a relief to executives who are always thirsty for something new and interesting, it presents two problems.

181

First, it derails the discussion of the more tactical issues that must be addressed during staff meetings. Second, it causes the team to take on critical topics in an environment where they don't have enough time to achieve resolution and when they are not as informed or prepared as they need to be. That's why leaders of a healthy organization must also have a third kind of meeting.

3. Adhoc Topical Meetings

Probably the most interesting and compelling of all meetings is the third type: the adhoc topical meeting. In fact, it may be the most fun that leaders can have at work.

The purpose of this kind of meeting is to dig into the critical issues that can have a long-term impact on an organization or that require significant time and energy to resolve: a major competitive threat, a disruptive industry change, a substantial shift in revenue, a significant product or service deficiency, or even a troubling drop in morale, among many others. Any of these issues would warrant more time, energy, and preparation than could ever be given during a regular staff meeting. In fact, it's difficult to imagine addressing any of them in less than a few hours. It easily takes that much time to frame up an issue, present even a cursory overview of basic research, brainstorm possible solutions, debate the merits of those solutions, and then come to a decision with real commitment.

And yet leadership teams rarely carve out enough time for this. Instead, they try to resolve important issues in fifteen-minute increments in between more tactical and administrative topics during a staff meeting. The result is not only suboptimal decisions, but an immense sense of frustration among leaders. That frustration is most directly the result of knowing that they're making bad decisions, but also a vague sense that they're not getting to do what they thought they were going to be doing when they chose their careers in the first place.

Let me make this a little clearer. When most people decide to go into business, they envision themselves sitting around a table with a group of colleagues, wrestling with difficult issues, and doing their best to make the right decisions by tapping into everyone's knowledge, experience, and intuition. This is what happens during case studies in business school, and there's no denying that it's fun. The only problem with case studies is that they're not real, and they leave people looking forward to the day when they can take on real issues and make real decisions with real consequences.

And then something bizarre happens: executives in the real world find themselves so inundated with daily e-mail and voice mail and administrative requirements that they rarely, if ever, set aside enough time for thorough, challenging, tense, dramatic, and fun conversations. It's really quite absurd.

It's like a baseball player working all his life and finally making it to the Major Leagues, and then spending all his time at batting practice without ever stepping up to the plate during a game. Or better yet, when he finally does come to bat in a game, he rushes through it so he can get done quickly and get back to batting practice. The high point of being a baseball player is playing in the games, and the high point of being a leader in an organization is wrestling with difficult decisions and situations. Truncating those high points just doesn't make sense.

> The high point of being a leader in an organization is wrestling with difficult decisions and situations. Truncating those high points just doesn't make sense.

What makes this particularly tragic is that it is simply the result of executives mistakenly convincing themselves that meetings are inherently bad. Thinking they're being efficient, they reduce the time they spend in meetings by cramming every discussion into one big staff meeting. What they're really doing

183

is ensuring that those staff meetings are going to be ineffective and that the most important conversations they should be having—topical, strategic ones—are cut short.

What leadership teams need to do—and this may be the single most important piece of advice for them when it comes to meetings—is separate their tactical conversations from their strategic ones. Combining the two just doesn't work and leaves both sets of issues inadequately addressed.

As for the timing of topical meetings, there is no prescriptive answer. After all, critical issues don't come up on any schedule. However, if a leadership team goes more than a month without a strategic meeting, something is probably wrong. Of course, when a team first adopts this new model of having separate meetings for specific strategic topics, there will almost always be a big backlog of issues that need to be addressed, so there will be an initial flurry of these kinds of meetings. Which is okay because, by definition, the topics warrant attention. And besides, no one is going to complain about spending too much time discussing critical issues.

4. Quarterly Off-Site Reviews

The fourth type of meeting that every leadership team needs to have is often known as the "off-site." The problem with these meetings is that too often they are nothing more than an expensive and extended version of the unproductive staff meeting. The purpose of them, like each of the others, should be unique and focused. In this case, that focus is all about stepping back from the business to get a fresh perspective, which is why it is best done away from the office.

Activities that should be addressed during these meetings include reviewing the organization's strategic anchors and thematic goal, assessing the performance of key employees, discussing industry changes and competitive threats, and of course, reviewing the behaviors of the team members in regard to cohesiveness. In essence, the off-site review is where the leadership team needs to step back and revisit the four disciplines covered in this book: team, clarity, communication, and human systems.

The timing of these meetings, unlike the others, is not really negotiable. Unlike the tactical staff meetings, which might take place weekly or biweekly, or the topical ones, which need to happen whenever an issue arises, off-site review meetings should occur quarterly. There is just something about doing this four times a year that makes sense. More frequently than that doesn't give a team enough time to make progress on critical issues and identify meaningful trends in the market or in the company. Less frequently usually means that people are going to forget about what they talked about at the previous meeting, which makes continuity difficult and progress unlikely.

Finally, of the four types of meetings, the quarterly review is probably the one that might call for the use of an outside consultant. It's often nice for the leader of the executive team to participate as a member and leave the organizing and facilitating to a trusted consultant.

TOO MUCH TIME IN MEETINGS?

Whenever executives challenge me about the practicality of having four different meetings on a regular basis, I ask them to add up all the time that they would spend in those meetings in a given month.

If we apply the model in the most time-intensive way possible (a full 10 minutes each day in check-in meetings, 2 hours each week in tactical staff meetings, 6 hours each month in topical meetings, and 2 days each quarter in developmental review meetings), the grand total of time amounts to about 1,500 minutes, or 25 hours per month.

Assuming a 50-hour workweek, that amounts to about 12 percent of our time. If you work just 45 hours per week, then it's 13 percent. That means even when we're spending the maximum amount of time at each meeting, something few teams need to do, more than 85 percent of our time is still available for whatever else we do.

Some leaders will point out that they are often on more than one team, which they believe would make this kind of model unworkable. Well, even if a person were on as many as three teams and if all three of those teams spent the maximum amount of time in their meetings (something that is highly unlikely), that would *still* amount to less than half their time. And when we factor in the amount of time they'll avoid wasting because they are actually focused on the right issues during their meetings, and eliminating all the interruptions that happen because they're out of sync with one another, the value they get from having more meetings, not less, increases.

Finally, it's worth asking, *What else should leaders be doing besides going to meetings?* E-mail? Analysis? Customer visits? Okay, there are certainly times and places for those activities. But a leader's first priority is to create an environment where others can do these things and that cannot happen if they are not having effective meetings.

But what about management? Don't leaders need to allocate a lot of their time to managing their people? While it's true that the single most important activity that a leader must do (outside of being a good team member) is managing his or her direct reports, much of that actually happens during meetings. Sure, they need to do some one-on-one mentoring, but that isn't usually what executives are hoping to do when they're arguing about having to spend too much time in meetings. The truth is, if executives are having the right kind of meetings, if they're driving issues to closure and holding one another accountable, then there is much less to do outside meetings, including managing their direct reports.

The thesis behind all of this is worth repeating: a great deal of the time that leaders spend every day is a result of having to address issues that come about because they aren't being resolved during meetings in the first place. That's why it's really hard for executives to make a credible case for spending less time in meetings, assuming those meetings are good ones.

Old Dog, New Tricks

A church-related services organization was experiencing problems internally and seeing that those problems were affecting
their clients. Among the many things the leader did to make his
organization healthier, he cited the restructuring of his leadership team's meetings as a key part of their overall organizational
transformation.

"I'm fifty-eight years old, and I would never have thought that
having more meetings would help productivity, but it actually did.
The meetings have made converts out of us all."

Of all the recommendations my firm makes to clients, the one that
is most consistently embraced and touted as having an immediate
impact on an organization is the adoption of the meetings model outlined here.

Finally, it's important to remember that at the end of every meeting,
with the exception of the daily check-ins, team members must stop and
clarify what they've agreed to and what they will go back and communicate to their teams. This is called cascading communication and
it is covered in detail in the Discipline 3 section.

CHECKLIST FOR MEETINGS

Members of a leadership team can be confident that they've mastered meetings when they can affirm the following statements:

— Tactical and strategic discussions are addressed in separate meetings.

— During tactical staff meetings, agendas are set only after the team has reviewed its progress against goals. Noncritical administrative topics are easily discarded.

— During topical meetings, enough time is allocated to major issues to allow for clarification, debate, and resolution.

— The team meets quarterly away from the office to review what is happening in the industry, in the organization, and on the team.

Seizing the
Advantage

The power of organizational health is undeniable. Even the most skeptical executives I meet don't dispute the advantage they could achieve if they could make their leadership teams more cohesive, align them around the answers to the six questions, and get them to communicate and reinforce those answers incessantly. Indeed a number of healthy organizations have already proven this. Yet the fact remains that organizational health is largely untapped in most companies. But that's going to change.

As more and more leaders come to the realization that the last frontier of competitive advantage will be the transformation of unhealthy organizations into healthy ones, there will be a shift in the mind-set of executives away from more technical pursuits that can be delegated to others and toward the disciplines outlined in this book. Whether that takes place over the next five, ten, or twenty years, I don't know. But it's coming.

For the early adopters of organizational health, the advantages that they will reap will be amplified as they achieve even greater differentiation from their lagging competitors. But there are a couple of factors that they must embrace in order to avoid experiencing false starts and undue cynicism. For one, they'll have to begin the process with a few activities that will give them the initial momentum they'll need to see it through. Even more important, the individuals who lead this process will have to understand exactly what's in store for them.

THE LEADER'S SACRIFICE

By now I've made the point numerous times that many of the ideas I advocate in this book are simple. Well, this next statement will rank right up there with the most obvious piece of advice yet: the person in charge of an organization's leadership team is crucial to the success of any effort to build a healthy organization.

As ridiculously simple as that may sound, I can't help but believe that many leaders still don't fully understand it. All too often they see the tasks related to organizational health as a set of activities that others can handle. Some do this because they want to demonstrate to their staff members that they trust them to do their jobs. That is noble. Others do it because they'd prefer spending time on things that they enjoy more. That's not so noble. In either case, the result is the same: an unhealthy organization.

There is just no escaping the fact that the single biggest factor determining whether an organization is going to get healthier—or not—is the genuine commitment and active involvement of the person in charge. For a company, that's the CEO. For a small business, it's the owner. For a school, it's the principal. For a church, it's the pastor. For a department within a company, it's the department head.

At every step in the process, the leader must be out front, not as a cheerleader or a figurehead, but as an active, tenacious driver.

When it comes to building a cohesive team, leaders must drive the process even when their direct reports are less than excited about it initially. And they must be the first to do the hardest things, like demonstrating vulnerability, provoking conflict, confronting people about their behavior, or calling their direct reports out when they're putting themselves ahead of the team.

The leader must also be the driving force behind demanding clear answers to the six big questions, even when everyone else wants

> There is just no escaping the fact that the single biggest factor determining whether an organization is going to get healthier—or not—is the genuine commitment and active involvement of the person in charge.

to end the discussion and just agree to disagree. They must be constant, incessant reminders to the leadership team about those answers, challenging them about everything from their behaviors in relation to the organization's values to their commitment to the team's rallying cry.

As tempting as it may be, leaders must not abdicate or delegate responsibility for communication and reinforcement of clarity. Instead, they have to play the tireless role of ensuring that employees throughout the organization are continually and repeatedly reminded about what is important. And they must be on guard against contradictory and inconsistent processes that can confuse employees and against bureaucracy that can creep into an organization when people get complacent.

If all of this sounds daunting, that's because it is. People who lead healthy organizations sign up for a monumental task—and a very selfless one. That is why they need to relinquish their more technical responsibilities, or even their favorite roles, that others can handle. Because when an organization is healthy (when the leader at the top is doing his or her most important job), people find a way to get things done. When an organization is unhealthy, no amount of heroism or technical expertise is going to make up for the confusion and politics that take root.

The truth is, being the leader of a healthy organization is just plain hard. But in the end, it is undeniably worth it.

FIRST CRITICAL STEPS

In order to give their organizations the best possible chance of succeeding in these efforts, a team must engage in a few vital initial steps to get momentum started.

The first of those is setting aside time to launch the process. What I'm talking about is an *initial off-site,* a couple of days away from the office—productive, intense, non-touchy-feely days—working on the first two disciplines of building team cohesion and creating clarity. At the end of those days, the team will emerge with a heightened sense of trust and collaboration (trust me, they will), as well as some solid, if not completely refined, answers to the six critical questions.

After that initial off-site, the team will need to put together a *playbook,* a short summary of those answers and a few other items related to how the team behaves and how it will go about working together going forward. And once the information in the playbook has been finalized and the answers fully agreed on by the team, the next step will be to properly communicate it to the rest of the organization. This will require some kind of *initial communication,* followed by ongoing reminders from leaders using every form of communication at their disposal. And finally, the leadership team will need to spend time, probably a fair amount of time, *designing systems* to reinforce the information from the playbook by embedding it into every process that involves people.

Every team, every organization, will go about the organizational health process in slightly different ways. And that's a good thing. A rigid, one-size-fits-all approach usually ends up fitting no one and makes it likely that teams will abandon a program because it becomes too onerous. However, these initial steps, which take anywhere from one to six months depending on how much time and energy leaders allocate, are absolutely essential. Once the leaders get through these steps, they will have created so much momentum that it will be hard for them to grow complacent and let the process atrophy.

Of course, their work is not over. It never is. Like a marriage, it requires ongoing attention and effort: maintaining a cohesive team, revisiting the answers to the six questions, overcommunicating and reinforcing them. But leaders in healthy organizations rarely lament having to invest time and energy in that effort. In fact, they almost always come to enjoy it because they see the extraordinary benefits it produces regardless of how simple or unsophisticated it may seem at first glance.

ULTIMATE IMPACT

Finally, it's certainly worth acknowledging that the impact of organizational health goes far beyond the walls of a company, extending to customers and vendors, even to spouses and children. It sends people to work in the morning with clarity, hope, and anticipation and brings them home at night with a greater sense of accomplishment, contribution, and self-esteem. The impact of this is as important as it is impossible to measure.

At the end of the day, at the end of our careers, when we look back at the many initiatives that we poured ourselves into, few other activities will seem more worthy of our effort and more impactful on the lives of others, than making our organizations healthy.

Members of a leadership team can gain a general sense of their organization's health and, more important, identify specific opportunities for improvement by completing the following checklist.

Discipline 1: Build a Cohesive Leadership Team

— The leadership team is small enough (three to ten people) to be effective.
— Members of the team trust one another and can be genuinely vulnerable with each other.
— Team members regularly engage in productive, unfiltered conflict around important issues.
— The team leaves meetings with clear-cut, active, and specific agreements around decisions.
— Team members hold one another accountable to commitments and behaviors.
— Members of the leadership team are focused on team number one. They put the collective priorities and needs of the larger organization ahead of their own departments.

Discipline 2: Create Clarity

— Members of the leadership team know, agree on, and are passionate about the reason that the organization exists.
— The leadership team has clarified and embraced a small, specific set of behavioral values.
— Leaders are clear and aligned around a strategy that helps them define success and differentiate from competitors.
— The leadership team has a clear, current goal around which they rally. They feel a collective sense of ownership for that goal.
— Members of the leadership team understand one another's roles and responsibilities. They are comfortable asking questions about one another's work.
— The elements of the organization's clarity are concisely summarized and regularly referenced and reviewed by the leadership team.

Discipline 3: Overcommunicate Clarity

— The leadership team has clearly communicated the six aspects of clarity to all employees.
— Team members regularly remind the people in their departments about those aspects of clarity.
— The team leaves meetings with clear and specific agreements about what to communicate to their employees, and they cascade those messages quickly after meetings.
— Employees are able to accurately articulate the organization's reason for existence, values, strategic anchors, and goals.

Discipline 4: Reinforce Clarity

— The organization has a simple way to ensure that new hires are carefully selected based on the company's values.

— New people are brought into the organization by thoroughly teaching them about the six elements of clarity.

— Managers throughout the organization have a simple, consistent, and nonbureaucratic system for setting goals and reviewing progress with employees. That system is customized around the elements of clarity.

— Employees who don't fit the values are managed out of the organization. Poor performers who do fit the values are given the coaching and assistance they need to succeed.

— Compensation and reward systems are built around the values and goals of the organization.

Meetings

— Tactical and strategic discussions are addressed in separate meetings.

— During tactical staff meetings, agendas are set only after the team has reviewed its progress against goals. Noncritical administrative topics are easily discarded.

— During topical meetings, enough time is allocated to major issues to allow for clarification, debate, and resolution.

— The team meets quarterly away from the office to review what is happening in the industry, in the organization, and on the team.

MORE RESOURCES

If you would like more information about the advantage of organizational health, visit our Web site at www.tablegroup.com/advantage. You will find a variety of resources including:

- Video clips that describe the principles of organizational health
- An organizational health survey to assess and guide your organization
- A road map to help with implementation
- Models that can be downloaded for reference
- An online publication with weekly articles and resources related to organizational health

Achieving organizational health is an ongoing process that takes work every day. If you would like someone to help you implement any of the concepts around organizational health, please contact us at The Table Group: 925.299.9700 or www.tablegroup.com.

NOTES

Introduction

1. *The Five Temptations of a CEO*, 1998; *The Four Obsessions of an Extraordinary Executive*, 2000; *The Five Dysfunctions of a Team*, 2002; *Death by Meeting*, 2004; *Silos, Politics, and Turf Wars*, 2006; *The Truth About Employee Engagement*, 2007; *The Three Big Questions for a Frantic Family*, 2008; and *Getting Naked*, 2010 (all San Francisco: Jossey-Bass).

Discipline 1: Build a Cohesive Leadership Team

1. P. Lencioni, *The Five Dysfunctions of a Team* (2002) and *Overcoming the Five Dysfunctions of a Team* (2005) (both San Francisco: Jossey-Bass).
2. J. Katzenbach and D. Smith, *The Wisdom of Teams* (Harper Business, 1994).
3. C. Argyris and D. Schön, *Organizational Learning: A Theory of Action Perspective* (Reading, Mass: Addison Wesley, 1978).
4. E. E. Jones and V. A. Harris, "The Attribution of Attitudes," *Journal of Experimental Social Psychology*, 1967, 3, 1–24; L. Ross, "The Intuitive Psychologist and His Shortcomings: Distortions in the Attribution Process," in L. Berkowitz (Ed.), *Advances in Experimental Social Psychology* (Orlando, Fla.: Academic Press, 1977).

Discipline 2: Create Clarity

1. J. Collins and J. Porras, *Built to Last* (Harper Paperbacks, 2002).
2. P. Lencioni, "Make Your Values Mean Something," *Harvard Business Review* (July 2002).

3. M. Porter, *Competitive Strategy* (Free Press, 1998).
4. M. Porter, "What Is Strategy?," *Harvard Business Review*, 1996.
5. P. Lencioni, *Silos, Politics, and Turf Wars* (San Francisco: Jossey-Bass, 2006).

The Centrality of Great Meetings

1. P. Lencioni, *Death by Meeting* (San Francisco: Jossey-Bass, 2004).

ACKNOWLEDGMENTS

The first person I want to acknowledge here is Tracy Noble, who has been deeply involved in shaping this book from day one. Your ability to jump from the big picture to the tiniest detail and back again is astounding, and your complete dedication is as appreciated as it is constant.

I also want to thank the rest of my colleagues and friends at The Table Group—Amy Hiett, Karen Amador, Jeff Gibson, Lynne Fiorindo, Alison Knox, Jackie Collins, Michele Rango, and Kim Loureiro—for their involvement, support, and passion. Working with you every day is a blessing in so many ways. And I want to acknowledge the Table Group Principal Consultants who add so much to our experience and to the impact that our firm is having in the world. You blow me away every time I see you and learn what you're doing out there.

Of course, most of all, I thank my wife, Laura, for her tireless dedication and commitment to me and our four boys. As the years go by, managing the family seems to get more challenging, and yet somehow you keep rising to that challenge. I really love you for that and for so many other reasons.

And I thank my four sons—Michael, Casey, Connor, and Matthew. I am so proud of the young men you're becoming, and I pray that I am being the dad you need and deserve.

I thank our many clients and customers who allow us to come into their organizations. Whether we're facilitating an executive off-site, delivering a speech, providing advice, or shipping you a product, know that we appreciate the trust you show us and honor what you are doing to improve your organizations.

A big thanks to my wonderful agent, Jim Levine, for your immersion in our world and your unsolicited ideas and suggestions that make us better every time we talk to you.

Thanks to my long-time editor, Susan Williams, and all her colleagues at Jossey-Bass and Wiley who have entered the fray with us again and again over the past fifteen years to ensure that we're delivering the best books we can.

I thank my many friends, especially John Beans, Father Daniel Massick, Jeff Gibson, Father Paulson Mundanmani, Matthew Kelly, Daniel Harkavy, and Ken Blanchard, for investing yourselves in me without counting the cost.

And of course, I thank my mom, for the birth thing and for still being a mom after so many years.

But above and beneath, around, and through all of this, I thank God—Father, Son, and Holy Spirit—for blessing me in so many ways and bringing me ever closer year after year. Your mercy endures forever.

ABOUT THE AUTHOR

Patrick Lencioni is founder and president of The Table Group, a firm dedicated to providing organizations with ideas, products, and services that improve organizational health, teamwork, and employee engagement. Lencioni's passion for organizations and teams is reflected in his writing, speaking, and consulting. He is the author of several best-selling books with over five million copies sold. When Lencioni is not writing, he consults to CEOs and their executive teams, helping them to become more cohesive within the context of their business strategy. The wide-spread appeal of Lencioni's leadership models have yielded a diverse base of clients, including a mix of Fortune 500 companies, professional sports organizations, the military, non-profits, universities, and churches. In addition, Lencioni speaks to thousands of leaders each year at world-class organizations and national conferences.

Patrick lives in the San Francisco Bay Area with his wife, Laura, and their four sons, Matthew, Connor, Casey, and Michael.

To learn more about Patrick and The Table Group, please visit www.tablegroup.com.